COMPAI TRAVEL GUIDE TO

FETHIYE, TURKEY

Must See, Must Do Activities! Top Attractions! insider and Local Tips! Cultural Immersion!

CARL DIAZ

COPYRIGHT NOTICE

This publication is copyright-protected. This is only for personal use. No part of this publication may be, reproduced, in any form or medium, stored in a data retrieval system or transmitted by or through any means, without prior written permission from the Author.

Legal action will be pursued if this is breached.

SCAN HERE TO GAIN ACCESS TO ALL MY BOOKS

DISCLAIMER

Please note that the information contained within this document is for educational purposes only. The information contained herein has been obtained from sources believed to be reliable at the time of publication. The opinions expressed herein are subject to change without notice. Readers acknowledge that the Author / Publisher is not engaging in rendering legal, financial or professional advice.

The Publisher / Author disclaims all warranties as to the accuracy, completeness, or adequacy of such information.

The Publisher assumes no liability for errors, omissions, or inadequacies in the information contained herein or from the interpretations thereof. The publisher / Author specifically disclaims any liability from the use or application of the information contained herein or from the interpretations thereof.

Table of Contents

DISCLAIMER 3
INTRODUCTION TO FETHIYE 11
   A Brief History. 11
   Fethiye at A Glance 16
Chapter 1 19
HOW TO GET THERE 19
   By Air: Nearest Airports and Flights 19
      Dalaman airport (DLM) 19
      Transportation from Dalaman Airport to Fethiye 22
   By Sea: Ferry Services 25
      Ferry Routes and Schedules 26
      Onboard Experience 27
      Arriving at Fethiye's Port 28
      Tips for a Smooth Ferry Journey 29
      Beyond Fethiye: Exploring More By Sea 30
   By Road: Bus and Car Routes 31
      Driving to Fethiye 31
      Bus Travel to Fethiye 36
   Making the Most of Your Journey 40
   Visa and entry Requirements 41
      Who Needs a Visa? 41
      How to Apply for A Visa 42
      Entry Requirements 44

Chapter 2 48
BEST TIME TO VISIT 48
   Seasonal Highlights 48
   Ideal duration of stay 50
   Personal Experiences and Tips 51
Chapter 3 53
TRANSPORTATION WITHIN FETHIYE 53
   Public Transport: Dolmuş and Buses. 53
      Dolmuş: The Local Minibus Experience 53
      Buses: The broader network 56
   Car Rentals 58
   Biking and Walking Options 65
      Biking in Fethiye 66
      Walking Around Fethiye 68
   Taxis and Ride-Sharing Services 72
   Practical Tips for Getting Around Fethiye 76
Chapter 4 79
TOP TOURIST ATTRACTIONS 79
   Telmessos Theatre 79
      Highlights of Telmessos Theatre 80
      Tips for Visiting Telmessos Theatre 82
      Nearby Attractions 83
   Tomb of Amyntas 83
   Kayaköy Ghost Town 88

- The churches ... 89
- The Houses ... 90
- The schools ... 90
- The chapels ... 91
- Practical information. ... 92
- Getting There ... 92
- Tips for visiting ... 93
- Nearby Attractions ... 94

Ölüdeniz Beach and Blue Lagoon ... 94
- The Beach ... 95
- The Blue Lagoon ... 97
- Tips for Visiting Ölüdeniz Beach and Blue Lagoon ... 99

Butterfly Valley ... 99
- Getting to Butterfly Valley ... 100
- Exploring Butterfly Valley. ... 101
- Tips for Visiting Butterfly Valley. ... 103

Saklikent Gorge ... 105
- Highlights Along the Way ... 107
- Adventure Activities ... 107
- Practical Tips for Visitors ... 108
- Nearby Attractions ... 109

Calis Beach ... 110
- Highlights of Calis Beach ... 111
- Tips for Visiting Calis Beach. ... 115

Chapter 5 117
ADVENTURE AND OUTDOOR ACTIVITIES 117
   Paragliding over Ölüdeniz 117
   Diving and Snorkeling 119
   Hiking the Lycian Way 120
   Boat Tours and Island Hopping 122
   Horseback Riding 123
   Jeep Safari 125

Chapter 6 127
CULTURAL EXPERIENCES 127
   Fethiye Museum 127
   Local Markets and Bazaars 128
      Fethiye Market 128
      Paspatur (Old Town) Bazaar 129
   Traditional Turkish Baths (Hamams) 130
      Old Turkish Bath 130

Chapter 7 133
ACCOMMODATION OPTIONS IN FETHIYE 133
   Luxury Resorts 133
   Boutique Hotels 134
   Budget Stays 136
   Vacation Rentals 137
   Choosing the Right Accommodation 138
   Booking Tips and Tricks 139

Booking Platforms 140

Chapter 8 141

DINING AND CUISINE 141

Traditional Turkish cuisine. 141

Top Restaurants and Cafés 143

Street Food and Local Delicacies 146

Vegetarian and Vegan Options 148

Chapter 9 151

ITINERARIES FOR DIFFERENT TRAVELERS 151

Weekend Getaway 151

    Day 1: Arrival and Exploration 151

    Day 2: Beach Day and Scenic Views 152

    Day 3: Adventure and Departure 154

Cultural Immersion Experience 155

    Day 1: Historical Sites and Local Flavors 155

    Day 2: Market Exploration and Cultural Workshops 156

    Day 3: Arts and Traditions 157

Adventure Seeker's Journey 157

    Day 1: High Adrenaline Activities 158

    Day 2: Water Sports and Hiking 158

    Day 3: Off-Road and On the Water 159

Family-Friendly Adventures 160

    Day 1: Fun and Relaxation 160

Day 2: Exploring Nature 161
Day 3: Educational and Entertaining 162
Budget Travel 163
Day 1: Affordable Exploration 163
Day 2: Nature and History 164
Day 3: Local Experiences 165

Chapter 10 167
SHOPPING AND SOUVENIRS IN FETHIYE 167
Local Handicrafts and Art 167
Best Shopping Areas 169
Tips for Bargaining 171
Personal Experience and Recommendations 172

Chapter 11 176
FESTIVALS AND EVENTS 176
Annual Festivals 176
Cultural Events and Performances 178
Public Holidays: 179
Other noteworthy events: 181

Chapter 12 183
PRACTICAL INFORMATION 183
Currency and Banking 183
Health and Safety Tips 185
Travel Insurance 186
Communication and Internet 187

Power and Electricity 188
Local Customs and Etiquette 189
Chapter 13 192
WHAT TO DO AND NOT TO DO 192
Respecting Local Customs 192
Safety precautions 193
Common Tourist Mistakes to Avoid 194
CONCLUSION 196
Preparing for Departure 196
Nearby Destinations for Further Exploration 196
Planning Future Visits 199
APPENDIX: USEFUL RESOURCES 202
Emergency Contacts 202
Medical Assistance 202
Police Stations 203
Embassy Contacts 203
Other Important Contacts 204
Maps and Navigational Tools 205
Additional Reading and References 206
Useful Local Phrases 208

INTRODUCTION TO FETHIYE

Fethiye is a gem nestled along Turkey's southwestern coast, a place where the azure waves of the Aegean Sea kiss the golden sands and history whispers through ancient ruins. When you walk into Fethiye, you get an immediate sensation of warmth, not just from the Mediterranean sun, but also from the dynamic energy that seems to flow from every corner of this wonderful town.

A Brief History.

Fethiye's rich tapestry of history makes it an endlessly fascinating place for travelers. This region has been inhabited for millennia, with each epoch putting its own imprint on the landscape. Here's a more in-depth look at Fethiye's history, which will help you appreciate this magnificent town even more.

Ancient Beginnings: Lycian Civilization

Fethiye, originally known as Telmessos, was one of the most important cities in ancient Lycia. The Lycians, noted for their distinct culture and advanced civilization, lived this area as early as the second millennium BC. Their unique rock-cut graves, carved into cliffs, are among the most visible remnants of their time. These tombs, particularly the Tomb of Amyntas, carved around 350 BC, have elaborate features and majestic decorations that reflect the importance and position of people buried therein.

The Lycians were also known for their federated system of governance, which was quite advanced for its time. They established a confederation of cities, each with its own authority but working together for mutual protection and cooperation. This Lycian League is regarded as one of the first examples of a republican form of government, influencing subsequent political systems, notably that of the United States.

Persian and Hellenistic Influence

In the 6th century BC, the Persian Empire, under Cyrus the Great, conquered Lycia, incorporating it into their vast domain. Despite Persian authority, Lycian culture and traditions persisted, and the region flourished as a cultural and commercial center.

Alexander the Great's arrival in Fethiye in the 4th century BC marked the start of another key chapter in the city's history. Alexander's conquest introduced Hellenistic influence, which combined with indigenous Lycian culture to form a distinct blend of traditions, art, and architecture. The city's prosperity persisted, and it became an important element of the Hellenistic civilization, promoting commercial and cultural contacts around the Mediterranean.

Roman era

Fethiye, previously known as Telmessos, joined the Roman Empire in the 2nd century BC. During the Roman period, the city experienced great prosperity and expansion. Roman architecture, including great temples, baths, and theaters, came to dominate the metropolis. Telmessos' historic theatre, located near the current marina, is an excellent example of Roman architecture. It could hold more than 6,000 people and was utilized for a variety of public events and concerts.

The city also benefited from the Pax Romana, a time of relative peace and stability in the Roman

Empire that allowed for trade and cultural interaction. Telmessos developed into an important port city, connecting the Lycian region to the rest of the Roman world.

Byzantine and Ottoman periods

Telmessos was incorporated into the Byzantine Empire following the fall of the Roman Empire. During the Byzantine period, Christianity grew and the city became a bishopric. During this time, several churches and religious sites were built, although many have since been destroyed.

In the 13th century, the region fell under the control of the Seljuk Turks, and by the 15th century, it became part of the Ottoman Empire. The Ottomans renamed the city "Makri" (meaning "distant" in Greek). Under Ottoman rule, the town flourished as a regional commerce and administrative hub.

In the late 19th century, the city was renamed Fethiye in honor of Fethi Bey, one of the first pilots of the Ottoman Air Force, who died in an airplane crash. This time also saw significant demographic shifts, particularly following the population exchange between Greece and Turkey in the 1920s, which brought many Turkish refugees from Greece to settle in Fethiye.

Modern era

Today, Fethiye is a thriving town that smoothly combines its rich historical past with modern conveniences. The wounds from a severe earthquake in 1957, which destroyed much of the old town, are visible. However, this disaster prompted enormous restoration efforts, resulting in Fethiye's current mix of ancient ruins and contemporary infrastructure.

Modern Fethiye has grown tremendously, thanks to its popularity as a tourist attraction. Its unique combination of historical sites, natural beauty, and genuine friendliness draws travelers from all over the world. Walking through Fethiye, you'll see vestiges of many eras, from Lycian graves to Roman theaters, Byzantine churches to Ottoman mosques.

The town's archaeological museum houses several items that provide glimpses into its rich history. Ancient Lycian inscriptions and Byzantine mosaics can be seen here, establishing a concrete connection to the many cultures that have called Fethiye home.

Fethiye's historical narrative is more than just one of conquest and change; it is also about perseverance and adaptation. Its capacity to maintain its distinct personality while embracing new inspirations is what makes it so remarkable. This rich historical backdrop enriches every encounter in Fethiye, transforming even a leisurely stroll through its streets into a voyage through time.

In conclusion, Fethiye is a living witness to the various layers of history that have influenced it. Each old tomb, crumbling theater, and cobblestone street tells a story about the civilizations that have left their imprint here. As you explore this fascinating town, you'll discover that Fethiye's history is more than just a backdrop; it's an integral, ever-present component of its charm and attractiveness.

Fethiye at A Glance

Modern Fethiye is a beautiful combination of the old and the new. The village is built around a natural port, where modern yachts bob softly beside historic Turkish gulets. Paspatur, Fethiye's ancient town, is a tangle of narrow lanes lined with shops selling everything from handcrafted crafts to the most recent fashion trends. You can enjoy a cup of Turkish tea in a modest café while watching the world go by.

The town's natural beauty is equally appealing. Fethiye provides a variety of outdoor activities, including the famous Blue Lagoon at Ölüdeniz Beach and lush hills and valleys for hikers and nature lovers. The Lycian Way, a long-distance trail winding across the countryside, offers some of Turkey's most beautiful views.

Fethiye is also a destination for adventure. Whether you enjoy paragliding from Babadağ Mountain, diving to explore underwater caves and wrecks, or relaxing on the beach, there is something for everyone.

Finally, there are the people. The locals of Fethiye are known for their hospitality. They greet guests with open arms, ready to share the beauty and history of their beloved town. This friendliness can be seen in every interaction, from a shopkeeper offering you a taste of lokum (Turkish pleasure) to a local fisherman telling sea stories.

Fethiye is more than simply a place; it's an experience, a trip through time, culture, and environment that will leave an unforgettable impression on your soul. So, let's dive deeper into what makes this place so special and why it should be at the top of your travel list.

Chapter 1
HOW TO GET THERE

When planning a trip to Fethiye, one of the most interesting aspects is determining how you'll arrive. This chapter will guide you through the numerous options, making your journey as smooth and pleasurable as possible. Whether you choose to fly, sail, or drive, you'll discover extensive information on the finest routes and services to make your trip to Fethiye a breeze.

By Air: Nearest Airports and Flights

For most travelers, flying is the quickest and most convenient method to get to Fethiye. Let's go into the details so you have all of the information you need to plan your flight properly.

Dalaman airport (DLM)

Dalaman Airport (DLM), about 50 kilometers from Fethiye, is the primary airport that serves the town.

Dalaman Airport serves as a significant international gateway to the Turkish Riviera, with connections to several European and Middle Eastern locations.

Airport Facilities & Services

Dalaman Airport is a contemporary facility that provides a variety of amenities to ensure a comfortable arrival and departure. Here's what to expect:

- **Wi-Fi Access:** The airport offers free Wi-Fi throughout, allowing you to stay connected and share your travel updates.
- **Currency Exchange:** There are various currency exchange counters and ATMs available, allowing you to readily purchase Turkish Lira upon arrival.
- **Dining Options:** The airport includes several restaurants, cafes, and bars that serve both local and foreign food. Whether you want a quick snack or a full dinner, there are lots of options.
- **Duty-Free Shopping:** Visit duty-free shops to buy souvenirs, cosmetics, electronics, and other products at tax-free prices.

- **Car Rentals:** Several well-known car rental companies, such as Avis, Hertz, and Europcar, have desks at the airport. Booking in advance can often result in lower rates and a larger selection of automobiles.
- **Information Desks:** There are information desks positioned throughout the airport that can assist you with your travel inquiries.

Flights to Dalaman Airport

Dalaman Airport is served by a number of airlines, including both scheduled and charter flights. Major airlines that fly to Dalaman include Turkish Airlines, Pegasus Airlines, EasyJet, Ryanair, and British Airways, among many others.

Seasonal flights

During peak tourist season (April to October), there are many more direct flights to Dalaman from other European locations. Airlines frequently increase flight frequency to meet rising demand. Outside of high season, you may discover fewer direct flights, with some requiring a layover in Istanbul or another large hub.

Booking Tips:

- **Book Early:** Flights to Dalaman fill up quickly, especially during the summer. Booking your tickets in advance can help you get better deals and more convenient flight times.
- **Flexible dates:** If you have variable travel dates, use fare comparison tools to discover the cheapest deals. Flying during the week or during off-peak hours can save you money.
- **Check baggage allowances:** Baggage rules vary among carriers. Check the baggage allowances and fees when booking your ticket to avoid surprises at the airport.

Transportation from Dalaman Airport to Fethiye

Upon arrival at Dalaman Airport, you have numerous options to reach Fethiye.

Shuttle buses

Shuttle buses are a popular and economical way to travel from the airport to Fethiye. Several firms provide regular shuttle service that coincides with airplane arrivals and departures. The travel takes approximately an hour and often costs between 25 and 35 Turkish Lira per person. Shuttle buses are comfortable, air-conditioned, and offer a straight route to Fethiye with few stops in between.

Private Transfers

Booking a private transfer is a more personalized and convenient choice. Many companies provide this service, which allows you to travel directly to your Fethiye accommodation with no detours. Private transfers can be scheduled in advance online or at the airport. Prices vary depending on the type of vehicle and number of passengers, but expect to pay between 150 and 200 Turkish Lira for a standard car.

Taxis

Taxis are readily available outside of the arrivals terminal. While they provide a quick and convenient option, they may be more expensive than shuttle buses or private transfers. A taxi ride from Dalaman Airport to Fethiye usually costs between 200 and 300 Turkish Lira, depending on the time of day and traffic conditions. Before embarking on your excursion, always agree on a fare with the driver.

Car Rentals

If you want to explore the region at your own pace, renting a car is a great option. Dalaman Airport has several international and local automobile rental firms. Booking in advance can often result in lower rates and a larger selection of automobiles. Driving in Turkey is generally uncomplicated, and the route from Dalaman to Fethiye is clearly marked. Depending on traffic, the travel takes between 45 minutes and an hour.

Public Transport

A public bus service connects Dalaman Airport to Fethiye for those on a tight budget. The HAVAŞ airport shuttle service runs regularly, aligning with flight schedules. Tickets can be purchased onboard, and the journey takes about an hour and a half. This option is more affordable, with tickets costing around 20-30 Turkish Lira, but it may take longer due to additional stops.

Tips for a Smooth Arrival

- **Prepare for Customs:** As with any overseas trip, be prepared to go through customs upon arrival.

Ensure you have your passport, visa (if required), and any other necessary papers ready.
- **Language:** While many people in the tourism business speak English, acquiring a few basic Turkish phrases can be helpful and appreciated by the locals.
- **Local Currency:** It's a good idea to keep some Turkish Lira on hand for modest expenses like bus fares or snacks. You can exchange money at the airport or withdraw cash from ATMs.
- **Emergency Contacts:** Save crucial contact information, such as your lodging and local emergency services, in case you require assistance upon arrival.
- **Travel insurance:** Ensure that your travel insurance covers all parts of your vacation, including medical emergencies and flight delays.

By Sea: Ferry Services

Arriving in Fethiye by sea is not only a beautiful way to begin your vacation, but it is also a one-of-a-kind experience that adds a sense of adventure and romance to your trip. Ferry services provide a convenient and scenic route from surrounding Greek islands, mainly Rhodes, to Fethiye. Here's everything you need to know to get the most out of your maritime cruise.

Ferry Routes and Schedules

Rhodes to Fethiye

The most popular sea route to Fethiye departs from Rhodes, a stunning Greek island in the Aegean sea. Several ferry companies serve this route, with daily or biweekly services depending on the season. The boat ride from Rhodes to Fethiye usually takes 1.5 to 2 hours. During the summer months, departures are more frequent to accommodate the increasing influx of travelers.

Book Your Ferry Tickets

Booking ferry tickets in advance is strongly advised, especially during the peak tourist season (June to September). Tickets can be purchased online from several ferry operator websites or at ticket offices in Rhodes and Fethiye. Dodecanese Flying Dolphins, Sea Dreams, and Blue Star Ferries are some of the most well-known ferry operators along this route. You may typically select your seat when buying online, and early bookings may result in cheaper fares.

Onboard Experience

Facilities and Comfort

The boats that travel between Rhodes and Fethiye are outfitted with luxurious interior and outdoor seating, allowing you to enjoy the ride in luxury. Indoor parts are air-conditioned, which provides relief from the heat throughout the summer months. Most ferries include a snack bar or café where you can buy drinks, sandwiches, and snacks. On some ships, you may discover duty-free shops selling local products and souvenirs.

Scenic views

One of the highlights of taking the ferry is the stunning scenery. As you depart Rhodes' harbor, you'll pass by the medieval city walls and the historic acropolis, which serve as a breathtaking backdrop. As the ferry approaches the Turkish coast, the Rocky Mountains and turquoise waters of Fethiye provide a magnificent backdrop. Make sure your camera is ready to record these moments.

Arriving at Fethiye's Port

Port Facilities

Fethiye's port is centrally positioned, making it convenient to begin exploring as soon as you disembark. The port area includes basic amenities such as bathrooms, a tourist information office, and taxi booths. You'll also find a few cafés and stores nearby where you can get a quick lunch or drink before traveling to your lodging.

Transportation from Port

When you arrive at the port, you have numerous alternatives for getting to your lodging or next destination:

- **Walking:** If your hotel or apartment is in the town center, you may opt to walk. Many hotels, restaurants, and stores can be reached on foot from the harbor.

- **Taxis:** Taxis are easily accessible at the port, making it a simple method to go to your hotel, especially if you have big luggage. Taxi costs are generally fair, but it's always a good idea to negotiate on a price before beginning your trip.
- **Public Transport:** For budget-conscious travelers, public buses (known locally as dolmuş) are an affordable option. There are bus stops near the harbor with lines that serve much of Fethiye. The buses run frequently and reliably, offering an authentic local experience.
- **Car Rentals:** If you prefer more flexibility, several car rental agencies have offices near the port. Renting a car allows you to discover Fethiye and its surroundings at your own pace.

Tips for a Smooth Ferry Journey

- **Check the Schedule:** Ferry schedules change based on the season and weather conditions. Always double-check departure times and arrive at the port at least 30 minutes before the scheduled time.
- **Travel Light:** Although ferries feature luggage storage, it is better to travel light for ease of movement. If you have bulky luggage, make sure it is placed safely in the designated spaces.

- **Weather Considerations:** Because the sea is unpredictable, it is best to check the weather prediction before embarking on your excursion. In the event of rough waves, ferry services may be delayed or canceled. A flexible itinerary might help with any adjustments.
- **Stay Hydrated and Protected:** Bring water and sunscreen, especially if you intend to spend time on the outdoor deck. The sun may be intense, so staying hydrated is critical throughout the summer months.

Beyond Fethiye: Exploring More By Sea

Once you arrive at Fethiye, you may be enticed to explore more of Turkey's coastline by sea. Several boat tours and cruises depart from Fethiye's port, offering both day trips and longer excursions to adjacent islands, isolated beaches, and hidden coves. Some popular boat excursions include:

- **12 Islands tour:** This full-day cruise visits some of the most beautiful islands in the Gulf of Fethiye, with lots of possibilities for swimming, snorkeling, and sunbathing.

- **Butterfly Valley and Blue Cave:** Nature enthusiasts can plan a day trip to the magnificent Butterfly Valley and the captivating Blue Cave.
- **Private Yacht Charter:** For a more personalized experience, consider chartering a private yacht. This allows you to explore the shoreline at your own speed, stopping wherever you like.

By Road: Bus and Car Routes

Driving to Fethiye or taking a bus can be a deeply enriching experience, allowing you to see more of Turkey's diverse landscapes and cultural sites along the way. Whether you're an adventurous road tripper or prefer the convenience and affordability of bus travel, this section provides all the information you need to make your journey to Fethiye as smooth and enjoyable as possible.

Driving to Fethiye

Driving in Turkey is generally straightforward, with well-maintained roads and clear signage in both

Turkish and English. Here's a detailed look at what you can expect on your drive to Fethiye from various major cities.

From Istanbul to Fethiye

The journey from Istanbul to Fethiye covers approximately 800 kilometers and takes about 10-12 hours by car. Here are some highlights and tips for this scenic drive:

Route Options:

- **Via Bursa and Izmir (E881/D650 and O-5):** This is a popular route that takes you through the beautiful Marmara and Aegean regions. You'll pass through historic cities like Bursa, known for its thermal baths and Ottoman architecture, and Izmir, a vibrant coastal city with a rich history.
- **Coastal Route (D400):** For those who prefer a scenic drive along the coast, the D400 offers stunning views of the Aegean and Mediterranean seas. This route is slightly longer but incredibly picturesque.

Stops Along the Way:

- **Bursa:** Visit the Green Mosque and Tomb, and enjoy a traditional Turkish meal at one of the local eateries.
- **Izmir:** Explore the Kemeralti Market, visit the ancient city of Ephesus nearby, and take a stroll along the Kordon, a scenic waterfront promenade.

Driving Tips:

- **Tolls:** Turkish highways have tolls, so ensure you have a HGS (Hızlı Geçiş Sistemi) sticker for automatic toll payment. These can be purchased at post offices (PTT) and some gas stations.
- **Rest Stops:** Turkey has numerous well-equipped rest stops along major highways, offering fuel, food, and restrooms.
- **Navigation:** While road signs are generally clear, having a GPS or a reliable map app can be very helpful.

From Antalya to Fethiye

The drive from Antalya to Fethiye is shorter, about 200 kilometers, and typically takes 3-4 hours. Here's what you need to know:

Route:

- **D400 Highway:** This is the main coastal road connecting Antalya to Fethiye. It's a well-paved road with beautiful sea views and occasional mountain landscapes.

Stops Along the Way:

- **Kemer:** A popular resort town with beautiful beaches and the ancient city of Phaselis.
- **Kaş:** A charming coastal town known for its crystal-clear waters and laid-back atmosphere. It's a great place for a quick swim or a bite to eat.

Driving Tips:

- **Scenic Views:** This route offers some of the most beautiful coastal views in Turkey, so plan for a few scenic stops.
- **Safety:** While the road is generally safe, be mindful of sharp bends and occasional steep sections.

From Ankara to Fethiye

If you're driving from Ankara, the capital city, the journey is approximately 630 kilometers and takes about 8-9 hours.

Route:

- **Via Afyonkarahisar and Denizli (D650 and D330):** This is the most straightforward route, passing through central Anatolia and into the Aegean region.

Stops Along the Way:

- **Afyonkarahisar:** Known for its thermal spas and delicious Turkish delight.
- **Pamukkale:** Famous for its white travertine terraces and ancient Hierapolis ruins, this is a must-see detour.

Driving Tips:

- **Road Conditions:** The roads are generally in good condition, but it's always wise to check for any construction or weather-related issues.
- **Fuel:** Gas stations are plentiful, but it's a good idea to keep an eye on your fuel gauge, especially when driving through rural areas.

Bus Travel to Fethiye

Turkey's bus network is extensive, offering comfortable and affordable options for travelers who prefer not to drive. Here's a closer look at taking a bus to Fethiye from major cities.

Bus from Istanbul to Fethiye

Duration and Frequency:

The bus journey from Istanbul to Fethiye takes about 12-14 hours. There are several bus companies offering multiple daily departures, especially during peak travel seasons.

Major Bus Companies:

- **Metro Turizm:** Known for its extensive network and comfortable buses.
- **Pamukkale Turizm:** Another reputable company with frequent services and good onboard amenities.

Onboard Amenities:

- **Comfort:** Modern buses feature reclining seats, air conditioning, and often entertainment systems.
- **Services:** Most long-distance buses offer refreshments, Wi-Fi, and USB charging ports.

Tickets and Booking:

- **Online Booking:** Tickets can be booked online via the bus company's websites or through travel agencies.
- **Pricing:** Prices are generally reasonable, with discounts often available for early bookings or off-peak travel.

Bus from Antalya to Fethiye

Duration and Frequency:

The bus journey from Antalya to Fethiye takes about 3-4 hours. Buses run frequently throughout the day.

Major Bus Companies:

- **Kamil Koç:** A well-known company with a reputation for comfort and reliability.
- **Bati Antalya:** A regional operator with frequent services along the coast.

Onboard Amenities:

- **Comfort:** Similar to other long-distance buses, you can expect comfortable seating and air conditioning.
- **Services:** Some buses offer light refreshments and Wi-Fi.

Tickets and Booking:

- **Stations:** Buses depart from the main bus terminal in Antalya, which is easily accessible by public transport or taxi.
- **Pricing:** Tickets are affordable, making bus travel a budget-friendly option.

Bus from Ankara to Fethiye

Duration and Frequency:

The bus journey from Ankara to Fethiye takes about 8-10 hours. Multiple departures are available daily.

Major Bus Companies:

- **Ulusoy:** A reliable company offering comfortable and punctual services.
- **Anadolu Ulasim:** Known for good service and well-maintained buses.

Onboard Amenities:

- **Comfort:** Expect reclining seats, air conditioning, and sometimes entertainment systems.
- Services: Refreshments, Wi-Fi, and power outlets may be available.

Tickets and Booking:

- **Convenience:** Tickets can be purchased online or at the bus station.

- **Pricing:** Reasonable fares, with discounts available for students, seniors, and advance bookings.

Making the Most of Your Journey

No matter which mode of transportation you choose, there are a few tips to ensure a smooth and enjoyable journey to Fethiye:

- **Plan Ahead:** During high travel seasons, it's a good idea to book your flights, ferries, or bus tickets ahead of time. This not only guarantees your position but may also save you money.
- **Pack Wisely:** Your means of transportation may require you to pack differently. Remember to check the luggage allowances for flights. If you're driving, make sure you have a decent map or GPS, and on ferries, pack a jacket because it might become cold on deck.
- **Stay informed:** Before you go, check the most recent travel advisories and weather conditions. This is especially critical for road travels, when conditions might change rapidly.
- **Relax and Enjoy:** The journey is part of the adventure. Take time to appreciate the sights,

whether from a plane window, a ferry deck, or an automobile. You'll have a sample of the breathtaking scenery that awaits you in Fethiye.

Visa and entry Requirements

Before you travel to Fethiye, be sure you understand Turkey's visa and entry requirements. This section will explain who need a visa, how to acquire one, and other important entry requirements to guarantee a smooth arrival in Fethiye.

Who Needs a Visa?

Turkey has different visa requirements depending on your nationality. Here's a general overview:

Visa-Exempt Countries:

Certain countries' citizens are exempt from visa requirements for brief stays in Turkey. These countries include Germany, France, Italy, Japan, and others. It is important to determine whether your country is on the list of visa-exempt nations.

E-Visa Eligible Countries:

Many travelers can apply for an electronic visa (e-Visa) before coming to Turkey. This easy online application is available to citizens of the United States, Canada, Australia, the United Kingdom, and many other countries. The e-Visa is normally valid for multiple entries and allows for stays of up to 90 days within 180 days.

Visa on arrival:

Certain nationalities can receive a visa upon arrival in Turkey. However, this option is becoming less prevalent, and travelers are advised to apply for an e-Visa in advance to prevent any border delays.

Regular visa:

Before traveling, nationals of certain countries must get a visa from a Turkish embassy or consulate. This lists countries that do not qualify for an e-Visa or visa-on-arrival.

How to Apply for A Visa

E-Visa Application

The e-Visa application process is simple and may be done online. Here's how.

- **Visit the official website:** Visit the official Republic of Turkey e-Visa website (https://www.evisa.gov.tr).
- **Fill out the application form:** Please include your personal information, passport information, and travel dates. Check that all information matches your passport perfectly.
- **Pay the Visa fees:** To pay the e-Visa charge, use your credit or debit card. Fees vary according to your nationality.
- **Receive your e-visa:** Once your application has been granted, you will get your e-Visa by email. Print a copy of the e-Visa to take with you when you travel.

Regular Visa Application:

For people who need to apply for a standard visa, there are numerous steps:

- **Gather the required documents:** Typically, you'll need a completed visa application form, a valid passport, passport-sized pictures, and

proof of travel plans. Depending on the type of visa you are applying for, you may need to provide additional papers.
- **Schedule an appointment:** To organize a visa appointment, contact your nearest Turkish embassy or consulate. Some embassies and consulates allow walk-in applications, but it is better to confirm ahead of time.
- **Submit Your Application:** Attend your appointment and submit your visa application with the necessary documentation. You may also have to pay a visa fee at this time.
- **Wait for Processing:** Processing timeframes vary, so apply well in advance of your anticipated travel dates. Once your visa has been approved, you must collect it from the embassy or consulate.

Entry Requirements

In addition to acquiring the necessary visa, there are various more entry requirements to consider before traveling to Turkey:

- **Passport validity:** Make sure your passport is valid for at least six months beyond your

planned stay in Turkey. This is a typical requirement for most foreign travel and helps to avoid complications at the border.
- **Proof of accommodation:** Be prepared to provide proof of your accommodations, such as hotel reservations or an invitation letter if you're staying with friends or relatives.
- **Return or Onward Ticket:** Immigration officers may ask to see proof of your return or onward travel arrangements. This helps to show that you don't plan to overstay your visa.
- **Sufficient funds:** You may be requested to give proof that you have enough money to support your stay in Turkey. This may contain bank statements, credit cards, or cash.
- **Health and Safety Measures:** Due to global health concerns, extra entry requirements such as proof of vaccinations or a negative COVID-19 test result may be required. Before you travel, be sure to check the latest health and safety advice issued by Turkish authorities.
- **Customs regulations:** Be aware of the customs rules for the products you can carry into Turkey. Certain items, including guns, drugs, and some technological gadgets, are restricted or forbidden. To avoid fines, declare all objects that need declaration.

- **Extend Your Stay:** If you want to extend your stay in Turkey beyond the duration of your visa, you have a few alternatives.
- **Residence Permit:** Apply for a short-term residency visa from the Directorate General of Migration Management. This is appropriate for those who want to stay in Turkey for longer than 90 days.
- **Visa Renewal:** In some situations, you can apply for a visa renewal or extension at a nearby immigration office. This option is subject to approval and is based on your unique circumstances.
- **Exiting and Re-entry:** If your visa permits for multiple entries, you can leave Turkey and return to reset your stay duration. However, this is only allowed provided your total stay does not exceed the permissible duration within 180 days.

Tips for a Smooth Entry

- **Prepare documents:** Keep all necessary paperwork organized and immediately accessible when you arrive at the border. This contains your passport, visa (if required), lodging information, return ticket, and any health certificates.

- **Be Honest and Polite:** Answer all immigration authorities' queries truthfully and pleasantly. Providing precise and succinct responses can assist speed up the entry process.
- **Stay informed:** Before you travel, check for modifications to visa and entrance requirements. Regulations can change, but staying aware helps ensure a smooth arrival.
- **Respect Local Customs:** Learn about Turkish customs and etiquette to demonstrate respect and make a good impression. Simple gestures, like as smiling while greeting people and utilizing simple Turkish phrases, can go a long way.

Conclusion

Understanding and meeting Turkey's visa and entry procedures is a crucial element of arranging your trip to Fethiye. By ensuring that you have the relevant visa, a valid passport, and all necessary documentation, you can enjoy your travel and the great adventures that await you in this stunning location. Safe travels and welcome to Fethiye!

Chapter 2
BEST TIME TO VISIT

Seasonal Highlights

When planning a trip to Fethiye, knowing when to go might make a big difference. I remember visiting Fethiye in the spring for the first time; the weather was great, and the countryside was ablaze with brilliant flowers. Each season lends its own unique appeal to this lovely seaside town, so let's have a look at what makes each season exceptional.

- **Spring (March to May):** Spring is my personal favorite time to visit Fethiye. The temperatures are warm, ranging from 15°C to 25°C (59°F to 77°F), making it ideal for outdoor activities such as hiking and seeing historic sites. The scenery is lush and green, with wildflowers covering the slopes. The weather is ideal for paragliding above the Blue Lagoon in Ölüdeniz, with favorable winds and clear skies.
- **Summer (June to August):** In Fethiye, summer is all about basking in the sun and relaxing in the warm, crystal-clear seas. Temperatures can

rise to roughly 35°C (95°F), making it an ideal time for beachgoers. Ölüdeniz Beach and Butterfly Valley are at their finest, with the water providing a pleasant retreat from the heat. Be prepared for greater crowds, though, as this is peak tourist season. If you appreciate water activities like I do, summer is an excellent season to go diving and snorkeling.
- **Autumn (September to November):** Autumn is another fantastic time to visit Fethiye. Temperatures range from 20°C to 30°C (68°F to 86°F) as the weather begins to cool down. The sea stays warm enough for swimming, and the crowds drop out, resulting in a calmer ambiance. The colder temperatures make long journeys more pleasant, making this a perfect season for hiking the Lycian Way. The local markets are likewise filled with fresh vegetables, making it a delight for foodies.
- **Winter (December to February):** Temperatures in Fethiye range from 10°C to 15°C (50°F to 59°F), which is milder than many other places. While not ideal for swimming, it's an excellent time to visit the town's cultural and historical monuments sans the summer throng. Winter is also the time to enjoy local customs and celebrations. I once went to a colorful

winter event at Kayaköy Ghost Town, which was a unique and unforgettable experience.

Ideal duration of stay

Deciding how long to spend in Fethiye might be difficult, but having spent a lot of time there, I can provide some tips to help you arrange the perfect trip.

- **Short Stay (3-4 Days):** If you have a limited time, a three to four-day trip to Fethiye can nevertheless provide you with a taste of the island's attractions. Spend the first day seeing the town and visiting ancient remains such as the Tomb of Amyntas. On the second day, visit Ölüdeniz Beach for a day of sun and sea. Reserve your third day for a boat tour of Butterfly Valley and the surrounding islands. If you have a fourth day, plan a brief trip to Saklikent Gorge for some adventure.
- **Medium Stay (5-7 days):** Spending a week in Fethiye allows you to explore more of the region's offers. For the first few days, stick to the short stay schedule, followed by a day hiking part of the Lycian Way. Include a visit to

Kayaköy Ghost Town, as well as opportunity to explore local markets and traditional Turkish spas. A day trip to the adjacent town of Dalyan, which has famed mud baths and old rock tombs, can also be beneficial.
- **Long Stay (10 days or more):** For those fortunate enough to have an extended stay, Fethiye offers endless possibilities. In addition to the foregoing activities, you may explore farther afield to destinations such as the historic city of Tlos and the breathtaking Patara Beach. Consider a multi-day sailing trip along the Turquoise Coast, where you may explore secret coves and stunning islands. With more time, you may engage in more leisurely activities, such as taking a cooking lesson to study Turkish cuisine or simply relaxing at one of Fethiye's many attractive cafés and restaurants.

Personal Experiences and Tips

Reflecting on my own visits to Fethiye, I remember one spring morning when I set out early to hike up to the Tomb of Amyntas. The walk was peaceful, and the air was cool and refreshing. As I reached the tomb, the view over Fethiye Bay was breathtaking, with the town still waking up below. It was one of those moments that felt ageless and profoundly rooted in the local history.

Another highlight was a boat trip to Butterfly Valley in late September. The summer throng had thinned, and we had the beach nearly to ourselves. The water was warm, and the nearby cliffs were filled with the fluttering wings of butterflies. It was like walking into a secret wonderland.

When planning your trip, my advice is to consider what type of activities you enjoy most and choose your travel dates accordingly. If you enjoy outdoor activities and prefer less crowds, spring and autumn are ideal. Summer is the best season to travel if you enjoy the beach and water activities. Winter, on the other hand, offers its own distinct appeal if you're looking for a more quiet experience with a focus on culture and local life.

Regardless of when you arrive, Fethiye's natural beauty, rich history, and warm friendliness will captivate your heart. Whether you're visiting for the first time or returning to explore more, each season provides unique amazing experiences in this charming corner of Turkey.

Chapter 3

TRANSPORTATION WITHIN FETHIYE

Before you begin discovering Fethiye's treasures, you must first learn how to get around. Let me walk you through the ins and outs of transportation in Fethiye, based on my extensive experience navigating this beautiful region.

Public Transport: Dolmuş and Buses.

Navigating Fethiye via public transport, particularly the dolmuş, is a practical experience with a hint of local character. Here's a detailed look at how to make the most of the dolmuş and bus services during your visit.

Dolmuş: The Local Minibus Experience

The dolmuş is more than simply a mode of transportation in Fethiye; it is a cultural experience that immerses you in the local way of life. These shared minibuses are a fixture in Turkish public transportation, and here's why they should be on your travel itinerary:

Routes & Destinations

Fethiye's dolmuş network is extensive, encompassing both the town center and the surrounding areas. The key routes include:

- **Fethiye to Ölüdeniz**: This is one of the most popular routes, taking you from the town center to the famous Ölüdeniz Beach. The trek takes around 30 minutes and provides stunning vistas as you descend into the turquoise ocean.
- **Fethiye to Hisarönü and Ovack:** These routes serve visitors to the busy resorts of Hisarönü and Ovack, areas famed for their active nightlife and diverse accommodations.
- **Fethiye to Kayaköy:** This route leads to the historic ghost village of Kayaköy, providing a glimpse into the region's past with its abandoned stone houses and narrow streets.
- **Fethiye to Calis Beach:** Take the dolmuş to Calis Beach, a long stretch of sandy and pebbly

beach with a promenade lined with restaurants and cafés.

Operating Hours

Dolmuşes often begin at 6:00 a.m. and go until midnight or later, particularly during the hectic summer season. During high tourist months, services are more frequent, so you'll never have to wait long for the next trip.

Fare and Payment

The fares for dolmuş rides are very affordable, making them an economical choice for getting around. Prices vary by distance, but most journeys cost between 3 and 10 Turkish Lira. Payment is straightforward: you simply hand your fare to the driver when you board. It's a good idea to keep little change on hand because dolmuş drivers may not have enough change for larger amounts.

Navigating the Dolmuş System

When using the dolmuş, here are some tips to make your journey smoother:

- **Boarding and Exiting:** Dolmuşes may be waved down along their journey, and passengers can request that the driver stop at any point along the way. Simply say "İnecek var" (I want to get off) when you reach your destination.
- **Signage:** Each dolmuş's destination is plainly posted on the front. If you're unsure, ask the driver or another passenger. The locals are typically quite helpful to tourists.
- **Comfort and Etiquette:** Dolmuşes may become congested, particularly during peak hours. Prepare for a comfortable travel, and always give your seat to senior people, pregnant ladies, or those with young children as a show of respect.

Buses: The broader network

For destinations beyond the reach of dolmuşes, Fethiye's bus system provides an efficient and reliable alternative. Here's all you need to know about taking buses:

Intercity and Local Buses

A network of intercity buses connects Fethiye to other cities and villages in Turkey. The main bus terminal (otogar) is located on the outskirts of the town, where you may take buses to significant places such as:

- **Antalya:** A popular route, with many buses every day transporting you to this lively coastal city noted for its ancient monuments and stunning beaches.
- **Mugla:** The provincial capital provides a more relaxed atmosphere with historic marketplaces and Ottoman architecture.
- **Izmir:** A little farther away, buses to Izmir give access to this dynamic city known for its cultural events and coastal promenade.

Local buses complement the dolmuş network by providing additional routes and services within Fethiye and the surrounding areas. They are particularly handy for accessing more rural sites or areas not served by dolmuşes.

Schedules & Tickets

Bus schedules are available at the bus station or online. During high travel seasons, it is best to purchase your tickets in advance, especially for longer interstate travels. Local bus tickets are typically bought directly from the driver, comparable to the dolmuş system.

Travel Comfort

Intercity buses in Turkey are renowned for their comfort and amenities. Most buses have air conditioning, comfortable seating, and, in some cases, onboard snacks and entertainment. It's an easy method to travel larger distances without the burden of driving.

Car Rentals

Renting a car in Fethiye offers up a world of options, allowing you to explore at your own leisure and venture into locations that may not be accessible by public transportation. Whether you're planning a day trip to a nearby attraction or a multi-day road trip down Turkey's magnificent southwestern coast, renting a car can greatly improve your vacation experience. Allow me to give some thorough thoughts and tips to help you get the most of your car rental in Fethiye.

Choosing A Car Rental Agency

Fethiye has a wide range of car rental options, from well-known international brands to reputable local agencies. Here are a few tips to help you choose the ideal one:

- **Research and Compare:** Before your trip, spend some time researching various car rental businesses online. Compare pricing, read customer reviews, and see what is included in the rental package. Websites like Rentalcars.com and Kayak can help you compare options.
- **Book in Advance:** To assure the best rates and availability, book your car rental in advance, especially during peak tourist seasons (June to September). Early bookings can result in discounts and a larger range of automobiles.
- **Local vs. international Agencies:** While international chains like Hertz, Avis, and Europcar are reputable, don't neglect local agencies like Xpress Rent a Car or Ege Rent. Local companies frequently provide competitive pricing and personalized service. Simply make sure to check their reputation through reviews.

Vehicle Types

Your travel objectives and tastes will determine the sort of car you choose.

- **Economy cars:** They are affordable and fuel-efficient, making them ideal for single travelers or couples. They are ideal for navigating city streets and short vacations.
- **Compact SUVs:** If you intend to explore more challenging terrain, such as mountain routes or seaside trails, a compact SUV offers superior handling and comfort.
- **Full-Size SUVs**: For larger groups or families, a full-size SUV offers ample space for passengers and luggage. It's also a fantastic option if you plan on driving lengthy distances.
- **Luxury Cars:** If you want to travel in style, consider renting a luxury car. While more expensive, they offer greater comfort and performance, making them ideal for a special trip.

Rental Costs and Insurance

Understanding the costs of renting a car will help you budget more effectively:

- **Daily Rental Rates:** Rental rates vary depending on the season, type of car, and rental duration. Expect to pay between €20 and €50 per day for an economy car, and €50 to €100 per day for an SUV.
- **Insurance Options:** While basic insurance is typically included in the rental fee, it is recommended to get additional coverage for peace of mind. Collision Damage Waiver (CDW), Theft Protection, and Personal Accident Insurance are popular options. Some credit cards provide rental car insurance as a benefit, so check with your issuer.
- **Additional Fees:** Be wary of any additional charges, such as airport surcharges, additional driver fees, GPS rentals, and child seats. To minimize surprises, please clarify these costs before booking.

Picking Up Your Rental Car

The process of picking up your rental car may differ slightly based on the agency, but here are the main steps to expect:

- **Documentation:** When you arrive at the rental office, you must produce your driver's license

(or foreign driving permission, if necessary), passport, and credit card. Ensure that the credit card has adequate credit to cover the deposit.
- **Inspection:** Before driving away, have a rental agent perform a thorough inspection of the car. To avoid arguments while returning the car, make a note of any existing damage on the rental agreement. Take photographs or video for your records.
- **Familiarize Yourself:** Take a few moments to familiarize yourself with the controls of the car, adjust the mirrors and seats, and activate the GPS if equipped. Make sure you understand how to control vital features such as the headlights, wipers, and fuel cap.

Driving in Fethiye

Driving in Fethiye and the surrounding areas is generally a pleasant experience; however, here are some tips to help you navigate safely and confidently:

- **Road Conditions:** Fethiye's roads are well-maintained, particularly the major highways and roads leading to famous tourist destinations.

However, some rural roads are small and winding, so drive with caution.
- **Traffic Rules:** Turkey drives on the right side of the road. Speed limits are usually 50 km/h in cities, 90 km/h on rural roads, and 120 km/h on highways. Always fasten your seatbelt and avoid using your phone while driving unless you have a hands-free system.
- **Parking:** Parking in Fethiye is very simple, with plenty of places accessible in most districts. Many sites have designated parking areas, and street parking is prevalent. Look for parking signs and be aware of any parking fines or restrictions.
- **Fuel Stations:** Fuel stations are plentiful, especially along major roads. Most have full-service options, with attendants refueling your car. Credit cards are commonly accepted, however it's a good idea to bring cash at tiny stations in remote areas.

Daytrips and Longer Journeys

A rental car allows you to go on a choice of thrilling day trips and longer journeys from Fethiye. Below are some of my top recommendations:

- **Saklikent Gorge:** Just an hour's drive from Fethiye, this breathtaking gorge provides trekking, river tubing, and a cool respite from the heat. The route takes you past charming villages and breathtaking scenery.
- **Patara Beach and Ruins**: About 75 minutes away by car, Patara boasts one of Turkey's longest sandy beaches and fascinating ancient ruins. Spend the day seeing the historical site and resting at the beach.
- **Kalkan and Kas:** These lovely beach towns are ideal for day trips. Kalkan is known for its stunning beaches and vibrant nightlife, whereas Kas has good diving opportunities and a more relaxed atmosphere.
- **Pamukkale:** A bit further afield, Pamukkale is about a 3-hour drive from Fethiye. It's well worth the trip to see the strange white travertine terraces and ancient ruins. Leave early in the morning to maximize your day.
- **Dalyan:** Approximately 90 minutes from Fethiye, Dalyan is famous for its river delta, ancient rock tombs, and the pristine Iztuzu Beach, a nesting ground for loggerhead turtles.

Returning your rental car

When it is time to return your rental car, follow these procedures for a smooth process:

- **Refuel:** Most rental agreements require you to return the car with a full tank of gas. To avoid refueling charges, refill at a nearby station before driving to the rental office.
- **Clean the Car:** While you are not required to have the car professionally cleaned, returning it in good condition is respectful. Remove all rubbish and personal items.
- **Final Inspection:** Allow time for a final inspection of the car with a rental agent. Ensure that all reported damages correspond to the first inspection report. Once cleared, you will receive confirmation that the car has been returned in good condition.
- **Documentation:** Keep all rental agreements, inspection reports, and invoices for your own keeping. These documents may be beneficial in the event of any future disputes or concerns.

Biking and Walking Options

If you, like me, prefer a slower pace, biking or walking around Fethiye is extremely satisfying. The town and its surroundings are naturally gorgeous, and exploring on foot or by bike allows you to take in the beauty while discovering hidden jewels.

Biking in Fethiye

Fethiye is becoming increasingly bike-friendly, with several rental shops offering a range of bicycles. Whether you want a normal bike, a mountain bike, or an e-bike, you'll find something to fit your needs. There are also dedicated bike paths, particularly along the coastline and in parks, which make for safe and scenic rides.

Best Bike Routes

The coastal path connecting Fethiye Harbor and Calis Beach is one of the most popular bike routes. This level, well-paved path is perfect for a leisurely ride, with spectacular views of the sea and neighboring mountains. Along the way, you can stop at one of the seaside cafés for a cool drink or a quick dinner.

For those looking for greater adventure, the trails around Kayaköy and the Lycian Way provide more demanding terrain. The Lycian Way, a well-known long-distance trail, includes sections appropriate for mountain biking. The path from Kayaköy to Ölüdeniz includes off-road riding and spectacular views. Prepare for some steep hills, but the work is well worth it.

Bike Rental Shops

There are various bike rental shops in Fethiye, mainly along the harbor and the town center. Prices are modest, and many shops provide hourly, daily, and weekly rates. Some popular rental stores include:

- **Fethiye Bike Rental:** Located near the harbor, this company rents out a range of bikes, including e-bikes, and includes helmets and locks with every rental.
- **Calis Beach Bike Hire:** This rental company is perfect if you want to explore the coastline path.
- **Ölüdeniz Bike Rentals:** Ideal for people staying in or around Ölüdeniz, this shop sells mountain bikes perfect for exploring the area's trails.

Safety Tips

While biking in Fethiye is typically safe, it is recommended to take the following precautions:

- **Wear a Helmet:** Always wear a helmet, even if it is not required. Safety should be a priority.
- **Stay Hydrated:** The Mediterranean environment may be fairly warm, so bring water with you, especially on lengthy rides.
- **Sun Protection:** To protect yourself from the sun, apply sunscreen and wear sunglasses.
- **Road Awareness:** Be careful of traffic, especially in congested places. Follow local traffic restrictions and use bike paths where available.

Walking Around Fethiye

Walking is another enjoyable way to explore Fethiye. The town is relatively tight, with several attractions located close together. While strolling through the old town, you may appreciate the historic architecture, visit local markets, and stop for a relaxing coffee at one of the many attractive cafés. For nature lovers, the coastal promenades and hiking trails provide stunning vistas and serene environments.

Top Walking Routes.

- **Fethiye Harbor to Calis Beach:** This picturesque promenade is perfect for an evening stroll. The path is flanked with palm palms and provides excellent views of the bay. It's a flat, easy walk that's appropriate for all ages.
- **Old Town and Fish Market:** Begin your tour in the old town, where you can explore small lanes lined with shops, cafés, and historic buildings. Make your way to the fish market, where you may eat fresh seafood at one of the nearby eateries.
- **Lycian Rock Tombs:** For a bit of history and a great view, hike up to the ancient Lycian rock tombs. The hike is short but steep, and the panoramic views of Fethiye and the harbor are well worth the effort.

Hiking Trails

Fethiye serves as an entrance to some spectacular hiking trails that combine beach and mountain landscapes. Here are some of my favorites:

- **Lycian Way:** This long-distance trail connects Fethiye and Antalya, going through some of Turkey's most spectacular scenery. You can hike shorter sections of the trail, such as from Kayaköy to Ölüdeniz or Faralya to Kabak, despite the overall length of over 500 kilometers. The trail is well-marked, so bring a map or GPS.
- **Kayaköy to Ölüdeniz:** This moderate hike takes you through the ghost village of Kayaköy and offers spectacular views of the coastline. The trail is approximately 7 kilometers long and takes 3-4 hours to complete. Make sure you wear sturdy shoes and carry lots of water.
- **Butterfly Valley:** Accessible by a short boat ride from Ölüdeniz, Butterfly Valley offers a beautiful hike through a lush gorge. The trail is rather short, but it can be steep and rocky in sections. The reward is a secluded beach with the opportunity to witness unique butterflies.

Walking Tours

If you prefer a guided experience, there are various walking excursions offered in Fethiye. These trips provide insight into the area history, culture, and natural beauty. Some prominent alternatives are:

- **Fethiye City Tour**: A guided tour of Fethiye's key attractions, including the ancient town, fish market, and Lycian rock tombs. The tour lasts approximately 2-3 hours and is an excellent way to become acquainted with the town.
- **Kayaköy Ghost Town Tour:** Visit the abandoned settlement of Kayaköy with a qualified guide who can tell you about its history and significance. This tour frequently includes a visit to a nearby winery or farm.
- **Lycian Way Guided Hike:** Those interested in hiking can take guided excursions along sections of the Lycian Way. These tours provide thorough trail information and ensure that you stay on the right path.

Accessibility

Fethiye is largely accessible to those with mobility impairments, particularly along the coastal promenade and in the town center. However, certain hiking trails and historical places may have uneven terrain or steep sections. If you have unique accessibility needs, you should check ahead of time and organize your journeys accordingly.

Taxis and Ride-Sharing Services

While traditional taxis are widespread in Fethiye, ride-sharing services are gaining popularity. These services provide a modern and convenient alternative for tourists who are accustomed to app-based transportation options. Here's a detailed guide on using ride-sharing services effectively in Fethiye, ensuring a smooth and stress-free experience.

Availability and popularity.

Unlike in other cities, ride-sharing apps such as Uber and Lyft are less common in Fethiye. However, there are local alternatives that cater specifically to the region. These apps may not be as well-known internationally, but they are highly appreciated by locals and sophisticated travelers alike. One such service is BiTaksi, which operates similarly to the global giants and offers reliable service throughout Fethiye and other parts of Turkey.

How to Use Local Ride-sharing Apps

To use these local ride-sharing services, you must first download the app from either the Apple App

Store or Google Play. Here is a step-by-step tutorial to help you get started:

- **Download and Install the App:** Look for BiTaksi or another local ride-sharing app in your app store. Download and install the app to your smartphone.
- **Create an Account:** Launch the app and create a new account. You'll need to enter basic information like your name, phone number, and email address. Some apps may ask you to verify your phone number by SMS.
- **Set Up Payment Options:** Most ride-sharing apps let you link a credit or debit card for cashless purchases. Some services may also accept PayPal and other digital payment options. Preparing ahead of time can save time and make the experience go more smoothly.
- **Enter Your Destination:** Once your account is set up, you can enter your destination into the app. The app will utilize GPS to locate you and display available drivers nearby.
- **Choose Your Ride:** Depending on the app and your location, you might have different types of rides to choose from, such as standard, premium, or larger vehicles for groups. Choose the ride that best meets your requirements and complete your booking.

- **Track Your Driver:** After confirming your ride, the app allows you to track your driver's whereabouts in real time. You will be given an anticipated arrival time and the option to communicate with the driver if necessary.

- **Enjoy the Ride**: Once your driver arrives, confirm your information, get in, and enjoy the ride. You can follow the route on the app and rest assured that you'll be brought directly to your destination.

Benefits of Using Ride-Sharing Services

Using ride-sharing services in Fethiye has various benefits:

- Convenience
- Cashless Payments
- Safety Features
- Transparent Pricing
- Language Barrier

Tips for a Smooth Ride-Sharing Experience

To make the most of ride-sharing services in Fethiye, keep the following points in mind:

- **Keep Your Phone Charged:** Make sure your smartphone is fully charged before leaving. Ride-sharing apps use your phone's GPS, and a dead battery can leave you stranded.
- **Check Driver Ratings:** Most apps show driver ratings and feedback. Choose drivers with high ratings for a better experience.
- **Verify Vehicle and Driver:** Before getting into the car, verify the vehicle's make, model, and license plate, as well as the driver's name and photo, to ensure you're getting into the right car.
- **Communicate Clearly:** If you have specific requirements or need assistance, communicate this to your driver in a friendly manner. Most drivers are eager to assist and make your travel enjoyable.
- **Leave Feedback:** After your ride, provide a rating and feedback. This improves the service for future consumers while holding drivers accountable for their actions.

Using Ridesharing for Airport Transfers

One of the most handy applications for ride-sharing services in Fethiye is airport transfers. Dalaman Airport is the closest international airport to Fethiye, and using a ride-sharing service might make your arrival and departure experience easier.

- **Book in Advance:** Some ride-sharing apps allow you to book rides in advance, ensuring that a car is waiting for you when you arrive. This is especially beneficial if you arrive late at night or during busy travel times.
- **Luggage Considerations**: Select a vehicle that can accommodate your bags if you're traveling with a lot of luggage. Many apps provide larger automobiles or SUVs for similar purposes.
- **Meet and Greet Services:** Some premium ride-sharing companies offer meet and greet services, in which the driver meets you within the airport with a sign. This might provide an extra degree of convenience, especially if you are new to the airport.

Practical Tips for Getting Around Fethiye

Once you've figured out how to navigate Fethiye, it's easy. Here are some practical ideas I've learned over the years to help make your trip smoother and more enjoyable:

- **Carry a Map or Download a Navigation App:** While the town is quite easy to traverse, having a map or a navigation app can be really useful, especially if you're heading into unfamiliar territory.
- **Learn Basic Turkish Phrases**: While many people in Fethiye understand English, knowing a few basic Turkish phrases will improve your experience and help conversations go more smoothly.
- **Stay Hydrated and Wear Comfortable Shoes:** Whether you're walking, riding, or utilizing public transportation, Fethiye's warm environment requires you to stay hydrated and wear comfortable shoes while exploring.
- **Respect Local Customs:** When using public transportation or cabs, be aware of local customs and etiquette. A nice smile and a polite demeanor can go a long way toward making your trip enjoyable.
- **Check schedules and Plan Ahead:** Especially for ferries and boat tours, check timetables

ahead of time and plan your trips to minimize last-minute problems.

Getting around Fethiye is part of the adventure and offers a chance to see the town and its surroundings from different perspectives. Whether you're taking a dolmuş, riding along the coast, or cruising the azure waters, each method of transportation brings a new dimension to your adventure.

Chapter 4

TOP TOURIST ATTRACTIONS

I've spent several days exploring every nook and cranny of this wonderful location, and I'm eager to share my discoveries with you. Let's get into the top tourist attractions that make Fethiye a must-see destination!

Telmessos Theatre

The ancient Telmessos Theatre, located in the heart of Fethiye, is a historical treasure that transports you back to the glory days of the Greco-Roman Empire. As you walk along its ancient stone steps, you can almost hear the murmurs of the past, filled with memories of big plays and gatherings. This well-preserved amphitheater provides not only a glimpse into history, but also breathtaking views of Fethiye's beautiful countryside.

Historical significance.

Fethiye was known as Telmessos in ancient times, and it was one of the most significant cities in Lycia. The theatre originated from the 2nd century BC, during the Hellenistic period, but it was later expanded by the Romans. It could initially seat approximately 6,000 people, indicating the city's importance and the cultural significance of theatrical performances in ancient times. The theatre hosted a variety of events, including plays, musical performances, and political assemblies.

Getting There

Address: Kesikkapı, 48300 Fethiye/Muğla, Turkey

The Telmessos Theatre is conveniently placed near Fethiye's city center, making it easy to get to whether you're staying or just visiting for the day. It's only a short walk from Fethiye harbor, so you can combine your visit with a leisurely stroll along the waterfront.

Highlights of Telmessos Theatre

Architectural Marvel

One of the most noticeable aspects of the Telmessos Theatre is its stunning architecture. The theatre is built into the hill's natural slope, taking advantage of the surrounding landscape to improve acoustics and stability. The seating is constructed in a semi-circular arrangement, as is customary in ancient Greek theatres, providing superb views and acoustics from every seat. As you go through the stone tiers, take a moment to admire the workmanship and engineering that have allowed this edifice to stand the test of time.

Panoramic views

The top tiers of the theatre offer stunning panoramic views of Fethiye, the azure seas of the Mediterranean Sea, and the surrounding mountains. It's an ideal location for photography, especially around sunset, when the entire landscape is bathed in golden light. Bring your camera to capture the breathtaking views as a keepsake of your visit.

Historical Interpretation

Information boards are strategically placed around the theatre, providing detailed explanations of its history, construction, and significance. These boards are incredibly educational, which helps visitors comprehend the context and appreciate the site even more. If you want a more immersive experience, try hiring a local guide who can share in-depth knowledge and fascinating stories about the theatre and the ancient city of Telmessos.

Tips for Visiting Telmessos Theatre

- **Wear Comfortable Shoes:** Because the theatre requires some climbing, it is recommended that you wear comfortable shoes, especially if you intend to explore the top stages.
- **Visit Early or Late:** Avoid the midday heat and crowds by arriving early in the morning or late in the afternoon. The lighting is also more favorable for photography during these times.
- **Bring Water and Snacks:** There are no facilities within the theatre itself, so bring water and some snacks to keep yourself hydrated and energized.
- **Combine with Nearby Attractions:** The theatre's proximity to the harbor makes it easy to combine with other sights like as the Fethiye Museum or a walk along the promenade.

Nearby Attractions

While you're here, take advantage of the nearby historical and cultural sites:

Fethiye Museum

Address: Kesikkapı, 505. Sk., 48300 Fethiye/Muğla, Turkey

The Fethiye Museum, a short walk from the Telmessos Theatre, housing an intriguing collection of artifacts from the Lycian, Roman, and Byzantine periods. The museum provides important context for the region's historical significance, with displays that include stunning mosaics, statues, and ordinary artifacts from ancient times.

Fethiye Harbor

The harbor is a lively place ideal for a relaxing stroll. You may watch boats bobbing on the water, get a drink at a waterfront café, or even arrange a boat tour to explore the nearby bays and islands.

Tomb of Amyntas

The Tomb of Amyntas is a site that sticks out when visiting Fethiye for both its historical significance and its pure architectural beauty. This ancient tomb, spectacularly carved into the cliffs above the current town, is a must-see for anybody interested in history and archeology.

Location and Accessibility:

The Tomb of Amyntas is located in the heart of Fethiye, Turkey. The exact address isn't necessary as it's well signposted and known locally, but for your GPS or map application, you can use: Kayaköy Mahallesi, 48300 Fethiye/Muğla, Turkey. It takes about 10-15 minutes to walk uphill from the town center. The trail is well-traveled but can be a little steep, so wear comfortable shoes and carry water, especially if you're visiting during the hot months.

Historical significance:

The Tomb of Amyntas, built in 350 BC, is a remarkable example of Lycian rock-cut tombs. It is named after Amyntas, Hermapias' son, an important character whose identity is still partly unknown. The Lycian civilization, famed for its distinctive funerary architecture, thrived in this area, and the tombs they left behind reveal their regard for the afterlife and artistic prowess.

Architectural Highlights:

What makes the Tomb of Amyntas particularly captivating is its façade, which resembles a Greek temple with its tall, fluted columns and intricately carved details. The accuracy and effort put into carving this tomb directly into the cliff face is incredible. The entrance is embellished with carvings that have lasted the test of time, demonstrating the artistry of old craftsmen.

What to Expect:

Upon arriving at the base of the cliff, you'll start your ascent via a stone stairway that winds its way up to the tomb. As you climb, you'll observe a number of lesser rock-cut tombs that, while impressive, lack the grandeur of Amyntas. The trek up provides progressively better views of Fethiye and its harbor, making it both scenic and historical.

When you arrive at the tomb, you will be struck by its overwhelming size. The tomb's scale is stunning, with massive columns and a huge entryway. Unfortunately, the interior is not open to the public, but the exterior is enough to make the visit worthwhile. Don't forget your camera; the area surrounding the tomb affords an excellent view point for photography.

Tips for visiting:

- **Best Time to Visit:** The tomb is open year-round, but the best time to visit is either early in the morning or late in the afternoon to avoid the midday heat and crowds.
- **What to Bring**: Comfortable walking shoes, a hat, sunscreen, and water are all necessary, especially in the summer. A camera is also required to record the breathtaking views and detailed intricacies of the tomb.
- **Guided Tours:** If you want to gain a better understanding of the site, try hiring a local guide. They can reveal fascinating insights about the tomb's history and significance, as well as the Lycian civilization.

Nearby Attractions:

The Tomb of Amyntas is close to several noteworthy sights in Fethiye. After your visit, you might wish to explore the Fethiye Museum, which is only a short walk away. The museum displays objects from the Lycian, Roman, and Byzantine periods, adding context to your visit to the tomb. Furthermore, the lively Fethiye Market and the gorgeous Paspatur (Old Town) are close, providing the ideal combination of history, culture, and local flavor.

Personal Reflections:

Standing before the Tomb of Amyntas, I was struck by the silent grandeur of this ancient monument. The sense of history is obvious, and the Lycian craftsmen's effort to carve such a masterpiece out of solid rock is quite impressive. The vista from the top, with Fethiye sprawled out below and the sea sparkling in the distance, will be with me forever. It's a place for contemplation, a somber reminder of the passage of time and the enduring legacy of human accomplishment.

To summarize, the Tomb of Amyntas is more than a historical site; it demonstrates the Lycian people's intellect and artistry. Whether you're a history buff, a photographer, or just a curious tourist, this renowned site will leave an indelible effect on you. Make sure to include time in your agenda to explore this remarkable piece of Fethiye's rich history.

Kayaköy Ghost Town

Kayaköy, also known as the Ghost Town, is an intriguing and hauntingly beautiful location that provides a sad peek into the past. Kayaköy, located around 8 kilometers south of Fethiye, was formerly a thriving Greek village until being abandoned in the 1920s during the Greek-Turkish population swap. Today, it is kept as a museum village, with vacant houses, churches, and streets telling the quiet stories of those who previously lived there.

Address: Kayaköy, 48300 Fethiye/Muğla, Turkey

Historical Context.

Kayaköy, previously Levissi, was home to a thriving Greek community. The population exchange that followed the Greco-Turkish War resulted in the displacement of Greek Orthodox Christians from Kayaköy to Greece, as well as Muslim resettlement in Turkey. However, many of the new residents chose not to settle in Kayaköy, leaving the village mostly abandoned. The abandoned stone homes, now overgrown with vegetation, serve as a melancholy reminder of this turbulent time in history.

Exploring the village.

When you visit Kayaköy, you will be taken back in time. The village, with its 350 or so houses, two churches, and numerous chapels, is remarkably well-preserved. Here are a few highlights you should not miss:

The churches

Lower Church (Panayia Pyrgiotissa)

The Lower Church, located at the village's entrance, is one of the first structures you'll meet. This Greek Orthodox church's beautiful stone construction has preserved some of its murals and elaborate decorations. The interior, however destroyed over time, conveys a feeling of the holy life that once flourished here.

Upper Church (Taksiyarhis Church)

Perched on a hill, the Upper Church provides a panoramic view of the village and surrounding environment. The journey to the church is hard, but the view from the top is well worth it. The church itself, albeit mostly destroyed, is a beautiful edifice with vestiges of its original frescoes and iconostasis.

The Houses

As you go around the village, you will note that the houses are tiered, following the natural curves of the slope. The architecture combines Greek and Turkish elements, with stone walls, wooden beams, and tiled roofs. Many of the houses still have their original doors and windows, and some even include pieces of furniture and household belongings. Walking through these empty streets and envisioning the lives of the individuals who previously called this place home is a weird experience.

The schools

Girls' School

The Girls' School ruins are located near the Lower Church. This building, once a center of education for the village's young girls, is now vacant, its classrooms and corridors resonating with memories of the past. It's a powerful reminder of the community's dedication to education and growth.

Boys' School

The Boys' School, located a little further up the hill, is another significant site. The building is larger and more imposing, indicating the importance of education in the village. The classrooms, which are now empty, provide a look into past educational processes and the daily lives of the village's children.

The chapels

Several modest churches may be found around the village, each with its own unique beauty. These chapels were originally the spiritual hub of the community, where residents gathered for prayers and celebrations. Though many of them are now in ruins, they nonetheless exude a sense of sacredness and peace.

Practical information.

- **Entry Fee:** There is a small entry fee to visit Kayaköy, which goes towards the preservation of the site. Tickets can be purchased at the entrance.
- **Opening Hours:** Kayaköy is open to visitors year-round. However, the best times to visit are in the milder months of spring and fall, as summer may be extremely hot.
- **Guided Tours:** To gain a better knowledge of the village's history and significance, consider taking a guided tour. Several travel organizations in Fethiye provide guided tours to Kayaköy.

Getting There

Kayaköy is easily accessible from Fethiye by car, bike, or public transport.

- **By Car:** If you're driving, follow the well-marked Kayaköy road from Fethiye. There is abundant parking at the village's entrance.

- **By Public Transport:** Dolmuş (minibuses) run regularly from Fethiye to Kayaköy. The trek takes approximately 30 minutes and provides lovely views of the countryside.
- **By Bike or Foot:** The more daring can rent a bike or hike from Fethiye to Kayaköy. The trail is well-marked and leads you through beautiful scenery and woodlands.

Tips for visiting

- **Wear Comfortable Shoes:** The ground in Kayaköy might be uneven and rocky, so wear strong, comfortable shoes.
- **Bring Water and Snacks:** There are a few small cafes and shops at the entrance, but it's a good idea to bring water and snacks, especially if you plan to spend a few hours exploring.
- **Respect the Site:** Kayaköy is a historical site that has been maintained. Respect the buildings and relics, and avoid climbing on them or removing anything.
- **Photography:** Kayaköy has wonderful photo chances, so don't forget your camera. The light in the early morning and late afternoon is really beautiful.

Nearby Attractions

- **Gemiler Island:** Just a short drive from Kayaköy, Gemiler Island is home to ancient Byzantine ruins and beautiful beaches. It's an excellent location for a picnic or a swim after touring Kayaköy.
- **Ölüdeniz Beach:** One of Turkey's most famous beaches, Ölüdeniz is not far from Kayaköy. Its turquoise seas and breathtaking scenery make it an ideal place to relax and unwind.

Ölüdeniz Beach and Blue Lagoon

Ölüdeniz Beach and the Blue Lagoon are the crown jewels of Fethiye, presenting incomparable natural beauty that attracts visitors from around the world. Let's go further into what makes this place so unique and provide you all the knowledge you need to make the most of your visit.

Ölüdeniz, which translates to "Dead Sea" due to its calm waters, is a small village and beach resort known for its stunning blue waters and scenic beauty. The beach is a long expanse of soft white sand that curves around the shoreline, with the gorgeous Blue Lagoon at one end. This area is a protected national park, therefore the pure environment is safeguarded.

Location and Access

Address: Ölüdeniz Mahallesi, 48340 Fethiye/Muğla, Turkey

Ölüdeniz is located approximately 12 kilometers south of Fethiye. It's easily accessible by car, taxi, or dolmuş (a shared minibus). If you are staying in Fethiye, you may board a dolmuş from the Fethiye bus station. It runs often and takes around 20 minutes to reach Ölüdeniz. The dolmuş service is inexpensive and provides a picturesque ride through the highlands and down the coastline.

The Beach

Ölüdeniz Beach is renowned for its clear, turquoise waters and gentle waves, making it ideal for swimming and sunbathing. The beach is divided into two areas: public and private beach clubs.

Public Beach

The public beach is open to everybody and spans along the coast, providing ample area to lay down a blanket and relax. There are sun loungers and umbrellas for rent, as well as shops providing snacks, drinks, and ice cream.

Highlights:

- **Swimming and Sunbathing:** The calm waters make it ideal for a relaxed swim.
- **Water Sports:** Kayak, paddleboarding, and banana boat trips are just a few of the accessible water sports.
- **Facilities:** The beach is well-equipped with restrooms, showers, and changing rooms.

Private Beach Clubs.

For an exclusive experience, visit one of the exclusive beach clubs along Ölüdeniz Beach. These clubs require an entrance fee but include amenities such as luxurious sun loungers, parasols, and full-service bars and restaurants.

Highlights:

- **Comfort and Luxury:** Enjoy a more comfortable environment with superior amenities.
- **Food and Drink:** Enjoy great meals and refreshing refreshments delivered directly to your sun lounger.
- **Activities:** Many clubs offer additional activities like yoga classes, beach volleyball, and live music events.

The Blue Lagoon

The Blue Lagoon is a breathtaking natural phenomenon located at the far end of Ölüdeniz Beach. It is well-known for its calm, crystal-clear waters, which provide an ideal backdrop for swimming and relaxing. The lagoon is part of a protected national park, which helps keep it in pristine shape.

Address: Ölüdeniz Mahallesi, Belceğiz Mevkii, 48340 Fethiye/Muğla, Turkey

Entrance Fee: There is a small entrance fee to enter the Blue Lagoon, which contributes to the conservation efforts of this beautiful area.

Opening Hours: The Blue Lagoon is open daily from 8:00 AM to 7:00 PM.

Activities & Highlights

- **Swimming and Snorkeling:** The calm, shallow waters of the Blue Lagoon make it ideal for swimming and snorkeling. The visibility underwater is great, allowing you to see a wide range of marine life, including colorful fish and the occasional sea turtle.
- **Pedalos and Kayaks:** For a fun and relaxing activity, rent a pedalo or kayak and explore the lagoon at your own pace. This is an excellent opportunity to enjoy the quiet waters while also getting a close look at the surrounding wildlife.
- **Nature Walks:** The Blue Lagoon area has numerous walking trails with breathtaking views of the lagoon and mountains. Take a leisurely stroll and experience the region's rich flora and fauna.
- **Sunbathing:** There are sandy and pebbly beaches around the lagoon where you may relax with a towel and enjoy the sun. The lagoon is usually less crowded than the main beach, providing a more relaxing atmosphere.
- **Facilities:** The Blue Lagoon area is well-equipped with facilities, including restrooms,

changing rooms, showers, and a few small cafes where you can grab a bite to eat or a refreshing drink.

Tips for Visiting Ölüdeniz Beach and Blue Lagoon

- Arrive Early
- Bring Sunscreen
- Stay Hydrated
- Respect the Environment
- Bring both Cash and Cards
- Safety first
- Plan for Sunset

Butterfly Valley

Butterfly Valley (Kelebekler Vadisi), nestled between towering cliffs and only accessible by boat or a strenuous hike, is one of Fethiye's most enchanting and hidden destinations. This natural refuge offers a distinctive blend of beautiful beaches, rich foliage, and an abundance of butterflies, making it a must-visit location for both nature enthusiasts and adventure seekers.

Getting to Butterfly Valley

By Boat

The most common and convenient way to get to Butterfly Valley is by boat. You may catch a boat from the nearby town of Ölüdeniz. Several boat cruises run everyday, particularly during the busy tourist season. The trip by boat is not only convenient, but it also offers breathtaking views of the coastline.

Boat Departure Point: Ölüdeniz Beach, Ölüdeniz, Fethiye, Muğla, Turkey

GPS Coordinates: 36.5485° N, 29.1234° E

By hiking.

For the more adventurous, hiking to Butterfly Valley is an option, albeit a difficult one. The trail starts in the town of Faralya, located above the valley. The hike can be fairly steep and demands a high level of fitness and prudence, particularly in some of the rougher sections of the trail.

Trailhead address: Faralya Village, Fethiye, Muğla, Turkey.

GPS coordinates: 36.5117° N, 29.1535° E.

Exploring Butterfly Valley.

The Beach

As you arrive, the first thing that will catch your eye is the stunning beach. The sand is soft, the water is crystal clear, and the scenery is simply magnificent. It's an excellent location for sunbathing, swimming, and snorkelling. The peaceful atmosphere and lack of large crowds make it an ideal place to relax and unwind.

The Waterfall

One of the main highlights of Butterfly Valley is the waterfall, located a short hike from the beach. The trail to the waterfall leads through lush flora and down the valley bottom, where you can frequently see many types of butterflies flitting about. The hike is pretty easy, taking approximately 20-30 minutes each way. The waterfall itself is a wonderful sight and an excellent place to calm down after a hike.

Camping

Camping in Butterfly Valley is an excellent choice for individuals who want to totally immerse themselves in nature. The valley features a rustic campsite where you can pitch your own tent or hire one on the spot. Spending the night under the stars, with the sound of waves in the background, is an incredible experience. The campsite also offers basic amenities such as bathrooms and a small café.

Campsite Contact: Butterfly Valley Camping, Faralya, Fethiye, Muğla, Turkey

Phone: +90 252 614 00 53

The Butterfly Valley is called after the many butterfly species that live there, including the Jersey Tiger (Euplagia quadripunctaria). The ideal time to see these butterflies is from June to September. Walking down the valley around this time will reveal many butterflies flitting around, creating a wonderful scene. It is critical to respect their habitat by not disturbing them and following the approved trails.

Activities

Aside from the natural beauty, Butterfly Valley offers a variety of activities to keep you entertained. Popular water activities include kayaking, snorkeling, and paddleboarding. Yoga sessions are also performed on a regular basis, allowing you to connect with nature and find inner peace in this serene environment. If you're interested in exploring the undersea world, the clean waters around the valley are ideal for snorkeling, allowing you to witness a diversity of marine species.

Tips for Visiting Butterfly Valley.

- **What to bring:** Water and snacks. The valley has minimal facilities, so bring your own water and snacks.
- **Sun Protection:** Because the beach offers minimal shade, bring sunscreen, a hat, and sunglasses.
- **Comfortable Footwear:** Whether you're hiking or exploring, comfortable shoes are essential.
- **Swimsuit and Towel:** The enticing waters will undoubtedly tempt you to take a dip, so be prepared.

Best time to visit

Butterfly Valley is best visited in the late spring and early autumn, between May and October. The weather is warm during this time, making it easier to spot butterflies. The valley can become fairly congested during the high summer months of July and August, but coming during the shoulder seasons can provide a quieter environment.

Responsible tourism

Butterfly Valley is a protected region, and visitors should preserve its natural beauty. To reduce your environmental impact, always carry your waste with you, avoid disturbing wildlife, and use authorized trails. The valley's allure resides in its pure condition, and it is up to each visitor to help keep it that way.

Local insights.

Chatting with the locals and the campsite staff can offer you with useful information and advice. They frequently have firsthand knowledge of the finest places to visit, the current state of the trails, and the ideal times to see butterflies. Their stories and experiences might enhance your visit and give you a better appreciation of the valley's history and significance.

Saklikent Gorge

Saklikent Gorge, also known as the "Hidden City" in Turkish, is one of Fethiye's most exhilarating natural wonders and a must-see for both nature enthusiasts and adventurers. Located around 50 kilometers from Fethiye, this deep, spectacular canyon is one of Turkey's longest and deepest, providing a one-of-a-kind and thrilling experience.

Getting There

Address: Saklikent Milli Parki, Seydikemer, Mugla, Turkey

Reaching Saklikent Gorge is quite straightforward. If you are staying in Fethiye, you can rent a car or take one of the many scheduled tours that include transportation. The drive takes around an hour and passes through stunning landscapes and charming communities. Alternatively, you can take a dolmuş (shared minibus) from Fethiye's major bus station to the gorge.

Exploring the Gorge

The entrance to Saklikent National Park is clearly marked and pleasant. The park itself has modest amenities like restrooms, tiny cafes, and gift stores. As you get closer to the gorge, you'll notice a delightful chill emanating from the small canyon, which provides welcome reprieve during the scorching summer months.

The Trek Inside

The journey begins as you cross a robust wooden suspension bridge that leads to the tight entrance of the gorge. From here, you must wade into the freezing waters of the Esen River. Water shoes are essential because the riverbed is rocky and the stream can be extremely strong. If you don't already have one, you can rent one at the entrance.

As you progress farther into the gorge, the towering cliffs climb abruptly on either side, reaching heights of 300 meters. The sheer scale and majesty of these rock formations are breathtaking, evoking the sensation of being in a natural cathedral. The path through the gorge is approximately 18 kilometers long, however most visitors only explore the first few kilometers, which are the most easily accessible.

Highlights Along the Way

- **Refreshing Pools and Waterfalls:** As you explore the gorge, you'll come across a number of natural pools and small waterfalls. These locations are ideal for taking a break and enjoying a refreshing plunge in the crystal-clear water.
- **Rock Formations & Caves:** The gorge is lined with remarkable rock formations and small caves, some of which are accessible. The play of light and shadow on the rocky surfaces contributes to the mystical aura of the location.
- **Wildlife and Flora:** Saklikent Gorge is home to a variety of wildlife, including birds, butterflies, and small mammals. The luxuriant foliage clinging to the rock walls provides color and vitality to the barren, rocky terrain.
- **Photographic Opportunities:** The dramatic scenery of Saklikent Gorge provides countless opportunities for photography. Whether you're photographing the towering cliffs, the rushing water, or the peaceful pools, you'll discover plenty of breathtaking images.

Adventure Activities

For those seeking an extra dose of adventure, Saklikent Gorge offers a range of activities beyond hiking.

- **River Tubing:** River tubing is a very popular activity. Float down the mild Esen River rapids while enjoying the scenery. It's a fun and relaxing way to calm down and see more of the gorge.
- **Canyoning:** If you're looking for a challenge, consider taking a guided canyoning excursion. These tours often involve climbing, swimming, and rappelling into the gorge's more remote and rugged areas. It's an exhilarating experience that provides a different viewpoint on this natural treasure.
- **Zip-Lining:** For a bird's-eye view of the gorge, take a zip-line across a part of the canyon. It's a brief but thrilling trip that allows you to soar over the river and admire the gorgeous surroundings from above.

Practical Tips for Visitors

- **Footwear:** Wear sturdy water shoes or sandals with good grip. The riverbed can be treacherous

and rocky, so adequate footwear is required for safety and comfort.
- **Clothing:** Wear lightweight, quick-drying garments. You will get wet, so avoid anything that will become heavy or uncomfortable once wet.
- **Sun Protection:** Although the gorge is sheltered in many places, the sun may still be harsh, especially at midday. Wear sunscreen, a hat, and sunglasses to protect your skin from the sun's rays.
- **Hydration and Snacks:** Bring a water bottle and some snacks. Although there are cafes at the entrance, it is a good idea to bring your own supplies, especially if you intend to spend several hours exploring.
- **Safety:** Always be aware of water levels and currents, especially after rain. Under these circumstances, the gorge might become more difficult and dangerous. It's best to go with a guide or a group, especially if you're not familiar with the area.

Nearby Attractions

If you have time, there are several other sights nearby Saklikent Gorge that are worth visiting.

- **Tlos Ancient City:** Located just a short drive from the gorge, Tlos is one of the oldest and most prominent Lycian cities. The site contains spectacular ruins, such as a fortress, rock-cut tombs, and an old theater, all set against a breathtaking mountain backdrop.
- **Patara Beach:** Known for its long stretch of golden sand and crystal-clear waters, Patara Beach is about an hour's drive from Saklikent. It's the ideal place to unwind after an exciting day in the gorge. The beach is also an important nesting area for loggerhead turtles.
- **Yakapark:** Located close to the gorge, Yakapark is a tranquil oasis featuring lush gardens, natural pools, and waterfalls. It's a nice place to have a relaxing meal and soak up the tranquil atmosphere.

Calis Beach

Calis Beach, famed for its laid-back atmosphere and breathtaking sunsets, is one of Fethiye's most popular locations. It offers the ideal balance of relaxation and excitement and is only a few kilometers from the town core. Here's an in-depth look at what to anticipate when you visit this stunning coastal destination.

Calis Beach runs about 4 kilometers down the coast, with a combination of pebbles and sandy regions. It's a popular hangout for both locals and tourists due to its calm atmosphere and spectacular views. The beach faces west, making it one of the best sites in Fethiye to observe sunsets.

Address: Foca Mahallesi 48300 Fethiye/Muğla, Turkey.

Highlights of Calis Beach

Promenade and Cycling Path.

The promenade parallel to the beach is dotted with cafés, restaurants, and stores. It's an excellent area to take a leisurely stroll while enjoying the sea breeze and bustling ambiance. One of my favorite hobbies was hiring a bike and going down the designated cycling path. The walk offers stunning views of the beach and the region, making it an enjoyable way to explore.

Sunset views.

Calis Beach is known for its stunning sunsets. Every evening, when the sun sets below the horizon, the sky becomes a canvas of bright colors. Many people congregate on the beach or in one of the coastal cafes to see this regular show. The ambiance is magical, and it's the ideal time to unwind with a drink and reflect on the day.

Water Sports and Activities

Calis Beach offers a variety of water sports for those looking for more adventure. You can attempt windsurfing, kitesurfing, and paddleboarding. The beach's consistent wind conditions make it especially popular with windsurfers. Several rental businesses and schools line the beach, providing equipment and lessons for both beginners and seasoned aficionados.

Cali Beach Bird Sanctuary

The Calis Beach Bird Sanctuary, located just beyond the beach, is a protected area where a variety of bird species live. It's a tranquil location for nature enthusiasts and birdwatchers. The sanctuary has a network of pathways and viewing sites, making it easy to explore. I spent the morning enjoying the tranquility and spotting some unusual bird species.

Seaside Restaurants and Bars

The seashore is bordered with a wide variety of dining alternatives, ranging from simple cafes to upscale restaurants. Many of these establishments include outside seating with spectacular views of the sea. Motto Dining (Address: Barış Manço Blv. No:40, 48300 Fethiye/Muğla, Turkey) is a popular seafood restaurant with a laid-back atmosphere. Guven's Restaurant & Bar (Barış Manço Blv. No:14, 48300 Fethiye/Muğla, Turkey) offers a variety of Turkish and international cuisine for a relaxed dining experience.

Accommodation Options:

Calis Beach offers a variety of accommodations to suit every budget. There's something for everyone, from luxurious resorts to low-cost motels and quaint guesthouses. Jiva Beach Resort (Address: Karagedik Mahallesi, 1112. Sokak, No:14, 48300 Fethiye/Muğla, Turkey) is a popular choice for those looking for an all-inclusive experience with top-notch amenities. Caretta Apart Hotel (Address: Barış Manço Blv. No:980, 48300 Fethiye/Muğla, Turkey) offers pleasant flats with kitchen facilities, ideal for families or extended visits.

Calis Market

Calis features a bustling market on Sundays that visitors to the area should not miss. The market offers a variety of things, from fresh vegetables and local delicacies to clothing and souvenirs, and is just a short walk from the beach. It's a terrific spot to find one-of-a-kind gifts or just hang around and enjoy the lively atmosphere.

Transportation

Calis Beach is quite easy to get to. It's only a 10-minute drive from Fethiye town center, and taxis and local dolmuş (minibuses) are easily accessible. The dolmuş to Calis Beach operates regularly throughout the day and is a cost-effective and convenient choice. If you are staying in Fethiye, you can take a beautiful water taxi from the town's harbor, which is a pleasant and picturesque way to get there.

Nearby Attractions

While in Calis, you can visit a number of other interesting attractions. The ancient city of Telmessos and the Fethiye Museum are only a short drive away. If you want to venture further afield, take a day trip to Saklikent Gorge or a boat tour of the stunning neighboring islands.

Tips for Visiting Calis Beach.

- **Sun Protection:** The sun may be very powerful, especially in the summer, so pack plenty of sunscreen, a hat, and sunglasses.
- **Footwear:** The beach contains both pebbly and sandy portions, so water shoes might help you navigate the pebbles comfortably.
- **Early Arrivals:** To guarantee a decent place on the beach, especially during high season, arrive early in the day.
- **Local Cuisine:** Don't miss out on trying some local Turkish dishes at the beachside restaurants. Fresh fish and mezes (small dishes) are highly recommended.
- **Wildlife:** Keep an eye out for the local wildlife, especially at the bird sanctuary. Bring binoculars if you enjoy bird watching.
- **Sunset Spots:** To get the finest sunset views, head to one of the beach's westernmost spots or arrive early at one of the beachside bars.

Calis Beach offers an excellent combination of relaxation, adventure, and local culture. You'll find plenty to keep you entertained, whether you want to chill with a book on the beach, participate in some exhilarating water sports, or explore the local market and bird sanctuary. It's a place where time appears to slow down, allowing you to fully immerse yourself in the beauty and tranquility of Fethiye's magnificent coastline.

Chapter 5

ADVENTURE AND OUTDOOR ACTIVITIES

Paragliding over Ölüdeniz

Paragliding over Ölüdeniz is a truly exhilarating experience that offers an unparalleled view of one of the world's most beautiful beaches. You will soar high over the stunning blue waters of the Blue Lagoon and the lush green mountains that surround it after taking off from the summit of Babadag Mountain, which stands at an amazing 1,969 meters (6,460 feet). The flight lasts between 25 and 45 minutes, depending on the wind and the flight path you choose.

Highlights
- **Spectacular Aerial Views**: Enjoy breathtaking vistas of the Blue Lagoon, Belcekiz Beach, and the surrounding mountains.
- **Thrill of Flight:** Feel the excitement of taking off from a high mountain and gliding through the air.

- **Photography Opportunities:** Take stunning aerial photos and films to remember your journey.

Practical information.

- **Best Time to Go:** The best months for paragliding in Ölüdeniz are from April to October when the weather conditions are most favorable.
- **What to Wear:** Comfortable, weather-appropriate clothing and durable shoes. Sunglasses and sunscreen are also advised.
- **Safety:** Paragliding firms in Ölüdeniz are well-regulated, with competent and certified pilots. Make sure you book with a reliable firm.

Recommended Companies

- **Sky Sports Paragliding**: Hisarönü Mahallesi, Ölüdeniz Caddesi No:25, 48340 Fethiye/Muğla, Turkey. https://skysports-turkey.com/tr/anasayfa/
- **Gravity Tandem Paragliding:** Ölüdeniz, Fethiye, Turkey. https://flygravity.com/en

Diving and Snorkeling

The crystal-clear waters around Fethiye are ideal for diving and snorkeling, revealing a rich underwater world alive with marine life. Whether you're an experienced diver or a beginner, there are several opportunities to explore underwater caverns, reefs, and shipwrecks.

Highlights

- **Aquatic Life:** You may see colorful fish, sea turtles, octopuses, and, on occasion, dolphins.
- **Dive Sites**: Explore prominent dive sites such as the Afkule Monastery, which has underwater caves, and the Kadirga Bay wreck.
- **Snorkeling Spots:** The Blue Lagoon and Butterfly Valley, which have shallow, clean waters, are great spots for snorkeling.

Practical Information

- **Best Time to Dive:** The diving season lasts from May to October, with the optimum visibility during the summer months.

- **What to bring:** A dive certification card (if you are a certified diver), swimsuit, towel, and an underwater camera.
- **Safety:** Make sure you dive with a licensed operator who offers proper safety briefings and equipment checks.

Recommended Dive Centers

- **European Diving Centre:** Çarşı Caddesi, 43 Sk, No: 4, Fethiye/Muğla, Turkey. https://www.europeandivingcentre.com/
- **Dolphin Diving Centre**: Belediye Marina, Fevzi Çakmak Cad, 48300 Fethiye/Muğla, Turkey.

Hiking the Lycian Way

The Lycian Way is a long-distance hiking trail that connects Fethiye and Antalya, traveling through historic ruins, lovely villages, and breathtaking coastline scenery. It's widely regarded as one of the world's top ten long-distance walks, providing hikers with a blend of cultural history and natural beauty.

Highlights

- **Stunning scenery:** Explore spectacular beaches, pine woods, and steep mountains.
- **Historical Sites:** Discover ancient Lycian tombs, Roman aqueducts, and Byzantine ruins along the way.
- **Village Life:** Discover traditional Turkish hospitality in small villages where you can stay in guesthouses and eat home-cooked meals.

Practical information.

- **Best Time to Hike:** Spring (April to June) and autumn (September to November) are ideal for hiking, with mild temperatures and blooming wildflowers.
- **What to Pack:** Comfortable hiking boots, layered clothing, a hat, sunscreen, a good quality backpack, and plenty of water.
- **Trail Markings:** The trail is clearly marked with red and white stripes. Maps and guidebooks are also recommended.

Recommended Sections:

Fethiye to Faralya: This section offers stunning views of the coast and passes through the Butterfly Valley.

- **Faralya to Kabak:** A beautiful hike that takes you through pine forests and along the cliffs, ending at the tranquil Kabak Bay.

Boat Tours and Island Hopping

Exploring Fethiye's coastline by boat is an amazing experience. Boat tours take you to isolated coves, pristine beaches, and picturesque islands where you can swim, snorkel, and relax in some of Turkey's most stunning scenery.

Highlights

- **Twelve Islands Tour:** A popular full-day tour that visits several picturesque islands and bays, including Tersane Island and Yassica Island.
- **Gemiler Island**: Known for its Byzantine ruins and stunning beaches, it's a great spot for a leisurely day of exploration and relaxation.
- **Swimming and Snorkeling**: Most tours include many stops for swimming and snorkeling in crystal-clear waters.

Practical information

- **Best Time for Boat Tours:** The summer months (June to September) are perfect, with mild weather and calm seas.
- **What to Bring:** Swimsuit, towel, sunscreen, hat, and snorkeling gear (if you have it).
- **Booking:** Tours can be arranged at the Fethiye marina or through your hotel. During peak season, it is recommended that you book ahead of time.

Recommended Operators:

- **Carole and Tayfun:** Located at Fethiye Marina, they provide a variety of boat tours and private charters.
- Blue Bays Travel: Offers a range of boat tours, including the popular Twelve Islands tour.

Horseback Riding

Horseback riding in Fethiye offers a unique way to discover the region's stunning landscapes, from pine forests and mountain trails to beach beaches. Whether you're an experienced rider or a beginner, there are alternatives to suit your skill level.

Highlights

- **Scenic Trails:** Ride through beautiful forests, along riverbanks, and up into the hills to get panoramic views of the area.
- **Beach Rides:** Take a leisurely ride along the beach and swim with your horse in the sea.
- **Cultural Experience:** Riding through traditional villages offers a glimpse into local life and culture.

Practical information

- **Best Time to Ride:** Spring and autumn offer the best weather for horseback riding, with cooler temperatures and blooming landscapes.
- Wear long pants, closed-toe shoes, and a hat for sun protection.
- **Safety:** The riding stables provide helmets, and the guides are qualified and knowledgeable.

Recommended Stables

- **The Ranch:** Located in Kayaköy, they offer a variety of riding tours and lessons.
- **Desperado Ranch:** Located near Çalış Beach, they offer beach rides and forest trails.

Jeep Safari

A jeep safari is a fascinating opportunity to explore Fethiye's challenging terrain and hidden gems. These guided tours take you off the usual road, past mountain villages, ancient ruins, and natural treasures.

Highlights

- **Off-Road Adventure:** Experience the thrill of driving through rough terrains, riverbeds, and forest trails.
- **Cultural Stops:** Visit traditional Turkish villages to learn about local customs and have home-cooked meals.
- **Natural Wonders:** Find hidden waterfalls, bathe in natural pools, and explore picturesque valleys.

Practical information.

- **Best Time for Safari:** Spring and autumn are ideal, offering comfortable temperatures and beautiful landscapes.
- **What to Bring:** Comfortable clothing, sturdy shoes, a hat, sunscreen, and a camera.

- **Safety:** Tours are conducted by experienced guides who prioritize safety and provide detailed briefings.

Recommended Operators

- **Volkan's Adventures:** Offers a range of jeep safari tours, including off-the-beaten-path routes. https://www.volkansadventures.com/
- **Saklikent Safari:** Specializes in tours to Saklikent Gorge and surrounding areas.

Fethiye is a playground for adventure enthusiasts, offering a wide range of activities that cater to different tastes and skill levels. Whether you're soaring above the Blue Lagoon, diving into the depths of the Mediterranean, hiking ancient trails, or exploring off-road paths, the region promises unforgettable experiences and memories. So pack your adventurous spirit, and get ready to explore the natural beauty and thrill of Fethiye!

Chapter 6

CULTURAL EXPERIENCES

Fethiye Museum

Address: Kesikkapı Mahallesi, 505. Sk., 48300 Fethiye/Muğla, Turkey

The Fethiye Museum is a hidden gem that provides an intriguing look into the region's ancient history. Despite its small size, the museum houses a significant collection of artifacts from the Lycian, Roman, and Byzantine periods. As you wander through the exhibitions, you'll see finely sculpted statues, intricate mosaics, and ancient pottery that depict the stories of the civilizations that once lived here.

Highlights:

- **Lycian Artifacts:** Explore treasures from the ancient Lycian civilization, such as intricate sculptures and inscriptions.
- **Roman and Byzantine Collections:** View statues, coins, and mosaics that highlight the rich history of these periods.

- **Ethnographic Section:** This section displays traditional Turkish artifacts, providing insight into the local way of life throughout the centuries.

The museum is conveniently placed near the town center, making it an ideal stop on any cultural itinerary. It's an excellent way to spend a couple of hours, especially if you're into history like I am.

Local Markets and Bazaars

Fethiye Market

Address: Cumhuriyet Mahallesi, 48300 Fethiye/Muğla, Turkey

Every Tuesday, the Fethiye Market explodes with color, sound, and aroma. This thriving market is a must-see for anyone looking to feel the energy of local life. As you go through the maze of vendors, you'll see everything from fresh fruits and vegetables to spices, linens, and handcrafted items.

Highlights:

- **Fresh Produce:** Try some of the juiciest fruits and vegetables you've ever had. Do not overlook the local olives and cheeses!
- **Spices and Herbs:** Bring home some of Turkey's best spices, ideal for replicating the flavors of your vacation.
- **Handicrafts:** Browse the stalls that sell wonderful fabrics, ceramics, and jewelry. These are great mementos or gifts for loved ones back home.

Paspatur (Old Town) Bazaar

Address: Paspatur Çarşısı, Cumhuriyet Mahallesi, 48300 Fethiye/Muğla, Turkey

Paspatur, Fethiye's Old Town, is a lovely neighborhood with tiny, twisting alleyways filled with stores and cafes. It's a great spot to explore and find hidden treasures. The bazaar here is smaller than the Tuesday market, yet it provides a more relaxing shopping experience.

Highlights:

- **Turkish Carpets and Rugs:** Paspatur is a great place to shop for traditional Turkish carpets.

Each piece is a work of art with its own individual story.
- **Jewelry:** Discover gorgeous silver and gold jewelry, typically with traditional Turkish motifs.
- **Leather Goods:** High-quality leather bags, shoes, and belts are plentiful in Paspatur.

Traditional Turkish Baths (Hamams)

Old Turkish Bath

Address: Cumhuriyet Mahallesi, 45. Sokak, No:4, 48300 Fethiye/Muğla, Turkey

When visiting Fethiye, it's customary to take a traditional Turkish bath, or hamam. The Old Turkish Bath in the town center provides an authentic and peaceful experience. These baths have been part of Turkish culture for generations and provide a unique way to relax.

Highlights:

- **Steam Room:** Begin your experience in the steam room, where the heat relaxes your muscles and opens your pores.

- **Body Scrub:** Next, you'll be given a thorough scrub with a kese (a special exfoliating mitt). This eliminates dead skin cells and makes your skin feel really smooth.
- **Foam Massage**: After the scrub, enjoy a luxurious foam massage. The bubbles and the masseur's skillful hands will relax any leftover stress.
- **Oil Massage:** For the ultimate in relaxation, book an oil massage at the end of your session.

Tips:

- You will get wet, so bring a swimsuit or a change of clothes.
- Relax and enjoy the experience; it offers a unique combination of relaxation and cultural immersion.

Fethiye's cultural experiences are diverse and enriching, with something for everyone. Whether you're roaming among ancient ruins, bartering at a local market, relaxing in a traditional bath, or tasting fresh seafood, there are endless ways to engage with the history and culture of this stunning region. So take your time, explore at your own pace, and immerse yourself completely in Fethiye's beauties.

Chapter 7

ACCOMMODATION OPTIONS IN FETHIYE

Luxury Resorts

When I think back to my time in Fethiye, I can't help but recall the splendid luxury resorts that dot the coastline. These resorts epitomize indulgence, offering every conceivable comfort and amenity. Imagine waking up in a plush bed, the soft murmur of the Mediterranean just beyond your balcony. You step outside to see a sprawling pool, perhaps with an infinity edge that seems to blend seamlessly with the sea.

- **Hillside Beach Club**

Address: Belen Cd. No:15, 48300 Fethiye/Muğla, Turkey

One of my favorite spots is the Hillside Beach Club, nestled in a secluded bay. The resort offers a private beach with crystal-clear waters perfect for a morning swim. The rooms are elegant, featuring modern decor with a touch of traditional Turkish charm. The resort also has several gourmet restaurants serving everything from fresh seafood to authentic Turkish cuisine. The highlight for me was the Serenity Beach, an adults-only haven where you can relax in a hammock strung between two trees.

- **D-Resort Gocek**

Address: Cumhuriyet Mahallesi, Gocek Koyici Mevkii, 48310 Göcek/Fethiye, Muğla, Turkey

Another gem is the D-Resort Gocek. Although technically in Gocek, it's close enough to Fethiye to merit a mention. This resort is all about understated elegance, with chic, minimalist rooms and a stunning marina view. They offer private yacht tours, which are an excellent way to explore the turquoise coast. The spa here is world-class, and I highly recommend the Turkish hammam treatment for a quintessentially local experience.

Boutique Hotels

If you're like me and enjoy something more intimate than a large resort, Fethiye has a charming array of boutique hotels. These places often have unique character and a personal touch that makes you feel right at home.

- **Yacht Classic Hotel**

Address: 1. Karagözler Mahallesi, Fevzi Cakmak Cd. No:10, 48300 Fethiye/Muğla, Turkey

One such place is the Yacht Classic Hotel. It's a small, stylish hotel right on the marina, with rooms that offer sweeping views of the harbor. The decor is modern but warm, with lots of natural light. What I loved most about this place was its rooftop pool and bar, perfect for unwinding with a cocktail as you watch the sunset over the boats.

- **Casa Margot Hotel**

Address: Karagözler Mahallesi, Fevzi Cakmak Cd. No:66, 48300 Fethiye/Muğla, Turkey

Another favorite is Casa Margot Hotel, perched on a hill with panoramic views of the bay. The hotel itself is a beautifully restored old house, with each room uniquely decorated. The atmosphere here is serene and refined, and the staff go out of their way to make you feel special. The on-site restaurant serves delicious Mediterranean dishes, and dining on the terrace with that view is an experience I won't soon forget.

Budget Stays

Traveling on a budget? No problem! Fethiye has plenty of options that won't break the bank but still offer comfort and a great location.

- **Hotel Letoon**

Address: Calis Plaji, 1054. Sk. No: 31, 48300 Fethiye/Muğla, Turkey

One such place is Hotel Letoon, located just a short walk from Calis Beach. The rooms are simple but clean and comfortable, and the staff are incredibly friendly. There's a nice garden area with a pool, perfect for relaxing after a day of sightseeing. Plus, being close to the beach means you can enjoy the stunning sunsets every evening without having to travel far.

- **Yildirim Guest House**

Address: 1. Karagözler Mahallesi, Bük Sokak No:3, 48300 Fethiye/Muğla, Turkey

Another great budget option is the Yildirim Guest House. This family-run place has a warm, welcoming atmosphere and offers basic but comfortable rooms. The location is fantastic, right in the center of Fethiye, close to all the main attractions. They also offer a complimentary Turkish breakfast, which is a lovely way to start your day.

Vacation Rentals

For those who prefer a home-away-from-home experience, Fethiye has an abundance of vacation rentals. These vary from small apartments in the middle of town to luxury villas with private pools in more remote locations.

One of my favorite stays was in a villa I discovered on Airbnb, nestled in the hills above Oludeniz. It had three bedrooms, a fully equipped kitchen, and a private pool with breathtaking views of the valley below. The calm and solitude were unparalleled, and it was only a short drive to both Fethiye town and the beach at Oludeniz. Staying in a villa allowed me the freedom to explore at my own speed while also providing the comfort of having my own space.

Example Villa

Address: Hisarönü Mahallesi, Likya Cd., 48340 Fethiye/Muğla, Turkey

If you prefer to be closer to the action, there are plenty of lovely apartments in Fethiye town. I once stayed in a beautiful penthouse apartment right on the marina, with two bedrooms and a spacious living area. The best part was the large balcony where I could sit with a glass of wine and watch the boats come and go.

Example Apartment

Address: Cumhuriyet Mahallesi, Çarşı Cd. No:10, 48300 Fethiye/Muğla, Turkey

Choosing the Right Accommodation

Choosing where to stay in Fethiye is primarily determined by your desired level of experience. If you want to be pampered and enjoy first-rate amenities, a luxury resort is the way to go. A boutique hotel provides a more personal and distinctive stay, with charm and character. Budget visitors will discover a variety of comfortable and reasonable options, and if you prefer solitude and flexibility, a holiday rental may be the best option.

Consider the location when arranging your stay. If you want to be close to the beach, Calis Beach is a fantastic location with numerous accommodation options. For those who prefer to be in the middle of the action, lodging in Fethiye town puts you close to shops, restaurants, and the marina. If you're looking for peace & quiet, the hills around Oludeniz have breathtaking views and provide a serene refuge.

No matter where you stay, Fethiye's lodgings cater to all preferences and budgets, assuring a comfortable and unforgettable stay.

Booking Tips and Tricks

- Book Early
- Flexible Dates
- Check Multiple Platforms
- Look for Deals and Packages
- Sign Up for Newsletters
- Use Reward Points
- Read Reviews
- Contact the Hotel Directly
- Consider Cancellation Policies

- Local Holidays and Events

Booking Platforms

- Booking.com - https://www.booking.com
- Airbnb - https://www.airbnb.com
- Expedia - https://www.expedia.com
- Hotels.com - https://www.hotels.com
- TripAdvisor - https://www.tripadvisor.com
- Trivago - https://www.trivago.com
- Agoda - https://www.agoda.com
- Kayak - https://www.kayak.com
- Orbitz - https://www.orbitz.com
- VRBO (Vacation Rentals by Owner) - https://www.vrbo.com

Reflecting on my numerous visits to Fethiye, I can confidently say that the variety of accommodation options is one of the town's strengths. Whether you're looking for luxury, charm, affordability, or privacy, you'll find the perfect place to stay. Each option offers its unique advantages, contributing to an unforgettable travel experience in this beautiful part of Turkey. So pack your bags, book your stay, and get ready to explore all that Fethiye has to offer!

Chapter 8
DINING AND CUISINE

Fethiye! Just thinking about it recalls so many flavors, fragrances, and fantastic dining experiences. If there's one thing that genuinely captures the essence of a place, it's its cuisine, and Fethiye is no exception. This chapter will serve as your culinary compass, guiding you through the pleasant and varied gastronomic landscape of this charming Turkish town. So have a seat at the table and let's go on this delightful journey together!

Traditional Turkish cuisine.

Fethiye's cuisine is a tapestry of rich, traditional Turkish tastes with a hint of Mediterranean spice. Many of the meals here are made with fresh, locally sourced ingredients. Vegetables, fruits, herbs, and spices all play important roles in creating foods that are both nutritious and delicious.

1. Kebabs & Grills

Kebabs are inextricably linked with Turkish cuisine. In Fethiye, you can find a variety of kebabs, one more tempting than the previous. Whether it's the delicious lamb shish kebab, marinated to perfection and grilled over an open flame, or the deeply spiced Adana kebab with its fiery kick, every bite is a flavor explosion. Doner kebab, a street food staple, consists of layers of seasoned meat shaved on a revolving spit and is typically served in a wrap or pita with fresh vegetables and a dollop of creamy yogurt sauce.

2. Meze: A Symphony of Flavors.

When you're in the mood to try a little bit of everything, meze is an important aspect of Turkish cuisine. These little, appetizer-sized dishes are ideal for sharing and typically come before the main course. Some must-try mezes are hummus, which is creamy and rich with the earthy taste of chickpeas and tahini; cacık, a refreshing yogurt and cucumber dip seasoned with garlic and mint; and dolma, filled vine leaves with rice, pine nuts, and currants. These are finest paired with a basket of freshly baked bread, still warm from the oven.

3. Seafood: Fresh from the Aegean

Given Fethiye's maritime position, seafood is plentiful and exceptionally fresh. Consider this: a seaside restaurant, the calm sound of waves lapping down the shore, and a platter of grilled octopus, wonderfully delicate with a slight sear and drizzled in olive oil and lemon juice. Or maybe you'd like a substantial seafood stew with mussels, clams, and chunks of fresh fish in a rich tomato sauce. Don't miss out on trying levrek (sea bass) or çupra (gilthead bream), which are commonly grilled and served with a wedge of lemon.

4. Pide and Lahmacun: Turkish pizzas

Pide and lahmacun are the way to go when you're in the mood for something comfortable and familiar while remaining authentically Turkish. Pide, also known as Turkish pizza, is a boat-shaped crust topped with a variety of ingredients such as minced meat, cheese, and vegetables. Lahmacun, on the other hand, is a thin, crispy flatbread filled with seasoned meat and baked till golden. Both are often served with fresh greens, tomatoes, and a splash of lemon.

Top Restaurants and Cafés

Now that we've whet our appetites with the fundamentals of Turkish cuisine, let's look at some of the greatest places to enjoy these delicacies in Fethiye. This town has everything, from sophisticated restaurants to small cafés.

1. Pasa Kebab

Address: Cumhuriyet Mahallesi, Atatürk Cd. No:48, 48300 Fethiye/Muğla, Turkey

Located in the heart of Fethiye, Pasa Kebab is renowned for its exceptional Turkish dishes, particularly its kebabs. The restaurant's friendly atmosphere and attentive service make it a favorite among locals and tourists alike. The mixed grill platter is a highlight, offering a taste of several different kebabs, including lamb, chicken, and Adana. Pair your meal with a glass of ayran, a traditional Turkish yogurt drink, for a truly authentic experience.

2. Mozaik Bahçe

Address: Cumhuriyet Mahallesi, 90/91 Sokak No: 43/B, 48300 Fethiye/Muğla, Turkey

Mozaik Bahçe is a hidden gem tucked away in a beautiful garden setting. The menu features a wide range of meze, along with delicious main courses such as lamb shank and grilled sea bream. The ambiance here is intimate and relaxing, perfect for a leisurely meal. Don't miss their baklava for dessert, which is often praised as the best in town.

3. Fish Market (Balık Pazarı)

Address: Cumhuriyet Mahallesi, Paspatur Çarşısı, 48300 Fethiye/Muğla, Turkey

For a unique dining experience, head to Fethiye's fish market. Here, you can choose your seafood from the market stalls, and one of the nearby restaurants will cook it for you. This bustling spot is great for enjoying freshly caught fish, squid, and shellfish. The atmosphere is vibrant and lively, with locals and tourists mingling over delicious food and wine.

4. Mancero Kitchen

Address: Karagözler Mahallesi, Fevzi Çakmak Cd. No:50, 48300 Fethiye/Muğla, Turkey

Mancero Kitchen offers a modern twist on traditional Turkish cuisine. Located by the marina, it provides stunning views to accompany your meal. The menu includes an array of dishes, from gourmet burgers and steaks to fresh seafood. The outdoor seating area is particularly lovely in the evening, with the sea breeze and the sound of boats in the harbor creating a serene dining experience.

5. Sezai'nin Yeri

Address: Foça Mahallesi, 48300 Fethiye/Muğla, Turkey

Sezai'nin Yeri is a family-run establishment known for its homestyle cooking. The menu features classic Turkish dishes prepared with love and care. The moussaka here is a standout, with layers of eggplant, minced meat, and béchamel sauce baked to perfection. This is the place to go for a hearty, comforting meal in a welcoming environment.

Street Food and Local Delicacies

Sometimes, the best culinary experiences come from the simplest places. Fethiye's street food scene is dynamic and diversified, with a variety of short snacks ideal for seeing the town on the go.

1. Simit, the Turkish Bagel

Simit is a popular street food snack that you can find on almost every corner in Fethiye. These sesame-crusted bread rings are somewhat chewy on the inside but crispy on the outside. They're ideal for a quick breakfast or mid-day snack. For a truly native experience, serve with a glass of çay (Turkish tea).

2. Midye Dolma (stuffed mussels)

Another must-try street food is midye dolma, often known as stuffed mussels. These are mussels stuffed with seasoned rice and herbs and served with a squeeze of fresh lemon. They are often offered by street sellers, particularly near the shoreline, and are an addicting snack that can be had on the go.

3. Lokma - Sweet Fried Dough

For something sweet, search for lokma, which are little dough balls that are deep-fried until brown and then drenched in syrup. These bite-sized delights are crispy on the exterior yet soft on the inside, making them an ideal dessert or snack. They are frequently sold from food carts and are best served fresh and hot.

4. Gözleme: Turkish crepes.

Gözleme is another popular street food, frequently prepared by women sitting on traditional griddles. These thin, savory crepes are filled with a variety of ingredients, including cheese, spinach, potatoes, or ground beef. They are then folded and fried till crispy. Gözleme is a delicious meal or snack that can be found at markets and street booths across Fethiye.

Vegetarian and Vegan Options

While traditional Turkish food is frequently heavy on meat, vegetarians and vegans have plenty of options in Fethiye. Turkish cookery makes extensive use of fresh vegetables, legumes, and grains, so there are plenty delicious plant-based dishes to enjoy.

1. Imam Bayildi: Stuffed Eggplant

Imam bayildi is a traditional Turkish meal that is suitable for vegetarians. It consists of eggplants stuffed with a mixture of onions, tomatoes, and garlic, all slowly cooked in olive oil. The end product is a thick, savory dish best served with a slice of crusty bread to soak up the delicious juices.

2. Mercimek Köftesi - Lentil Patties

Mercimek köftesi are spicy lentil patties cooked from red lentils, bulgur wheat, and a variety of herbs and spices. They are typically served chilled, with a touch of lemon and a side of fresh greens. These patties are healthful and tasty, making them ideal for a light dinner or appetizer.

3. Zeytinyağlı Dishes

Zeytinyağlı is a category of Turkish dishes fried in olive oil and served cold as part of a meze spread. Green beans, artichokes, and stuffed grape leaves are among the most common ingredients. These dishes are often vegan and emphasize the natural tastes of the veggies through the gentle richness of olive oil.

4. Vegan Restaurants and Cafés.

Fethiye has various vegetarian and vegan restaurants. The Vegan Market and Café, for example, serves a variety of plant-based dishes ranging from robust soups and salads to delicious sweets. Another excellent option is Yengen Burger, which is known for its creative vegan burgers and wraps.

- *Vegan Market and Café: Çalış Plajı, 48300 Fethiye/Muğla, Turkey*
- *Yengen Burger: Cumhuriyet Mahallesi, 40. Sokak No:3, 48300 Fethiye/Muğla, Turkey*

Fethiye's dining and culinary scene is a vibrant tapestry of flavors, textures, and scents that represent the town's cultural legacy and natural abundance. Whether you're eating a traditional kebab at a local restaurant, enjoying fresh seafood by the sea, or indulging in street cuisine delights, every meal in Fethiye provides an opportunity to connect with the heart and soul of this lovely region. So, let your taste buds guide you and enjoy the culinary journey that awaits you in Fethiye.

Chapter 9

ITINERARIES FOR DIFFERENT TRAVELERS

Whether you're traveling with family, looking for adrenaline-pumping activities, enjoying a romantic break with your significant other, or starting on a solitary journey of self-discovery, Fethiye has something special for everyone. This charming Turkish town, with its rich history, breathtaking natural settings, and vibrant culture, is a treasure waiting to be discovered. I have spent a lot of time wandering its streets, relaxing on its beaches, and learning about its history, and I can guarantee you that Fethiye never disappoints. Here's a full guide to creating the ideal itinerary based on your travel preferences.

Weekend Getaway

Day 1: Arrival and Exploration

Morning

Start your weekend in Fethiye with a hearty Turkish breakfast at Kale Park, where you can enjoy panoramic views of the town and the bay. Savor local delights like menemen (scrambled eggs with tomatoes and peppers) and fresh bread with honey.

Afternoon

After breakfast, take a leisurely stroll through the Fethiye Old Town (Paspatur). This area is rich in history and culture, with its narrow streets lined with shops selling everything from Turkish rugs to spices. Don't forget to visit the Fethiye Museum to get a sense of the local history and archaeology.

Evening

As the sun sets, make your way to Fethiye Harbor for a relaxing evening. The harbor area is bustling with life and offers plenty of dining options. Enjoy a seafood dinner at Mori Restaurant, where the catch of the day is always fresh and delicious.

Day 2: Beach Day and Scenic Views

Morning

Kick off your second day with a visit to Ölüdeniz Beach. This world-famous beach is known for its stunning turquoise waters and is perfect for swimming or just lounging under the sun. The Blue Lagoon nearby is a must-see, offering calm, clear waters ideal for a relaxing morning.

Afternoon

After a morning at the beach, head to Kayaköy Ghost Town. This abandoned village offers a fascinating glimpse into the past and provides plenty of opportunities for exploration. Take your time wandering through the old stone houses and churches.

Evening

For dinner, head back to Fethiye and enjoy a meal at Mozaik Bahçe. This restaurant offers a beautiful garden setting and serves up some of the best traditional Turkish dishes in town. Finish your day with a stroll along the harbor to soak in the evening ambiance.

Day 3: Adventure and Departure

Morning

Start your final day with a bit of adventure. Book a paragliding session over Ölüdeniz for an unforgettable experience. The views from above are absolutely breathtaking and provide a unique perspective of the area.

Afternoon

After your thrilling morning, unwind with a visit to Saklıkent Gorge. This natural wonder is one of the deepest canyons in Turkey and offers cool, refreshing waters to wade in and beautiful scenery to admire. Enjoy a light lunch at one of the local eateries near the gorge.

Evening

Before you depart, have a final meal at Mancero Kitchen. This waterfront restaurant offers a fantastic view of the sunset over the bay, making it the perfect end to your weekend getaway in Fethiye.

Cultural Immersion Experience

Day 1: Historical Sites and Local Flavors

Morning

Begin your cultural immersion with a visit to the Tomb of Amyntas. This ancient Lycian tomb carved into the cliffs offers impressive views of Fethiye and a peek into its rich history.

Afternoon

After exploring the tomb, make your way to Kayaköy Ghost Town for a deeper dive into the area's past. Wander through the eerie, abandoned buildings and imagine what life was like in this once-thriving community.

Evening

For dinner, experience a traditional Turkish meal at Oztoklu Restaurant. Try local dishes like kebabs, mezes, and baklava while enjoying live Turkish music.

Day 2: Market Exploration and Cultural Workshops

Morning

Start your day with a visit to the Fethiye Market. This bustling market is the perfect place to immerse yourself in local life. Browse stalls selling fresh produce, spices, textiles, and more. Don't forget to try some gözleme (Turkish pancakes) for breakfast.

Afternoon

In the afternoon, join a Turkish cooking class. Learn how to prepare traditional dishes like dolma (stuffed grape leaves) and baklava. This hands-on experience is both fun and educational, giving you a deeper appreciation for Turkish cuisine.

Evening

After your cooking class, enjoy a meal at Yengec Restaurant. This spot offers a cozy atmosphere and delicious local dishes, making it a great place to unwind after a day of cultural exploration.

Day 3: Arts and Traditions

Morning

Dedicate your morning to exploring Fethiye's art scene. Visit local galleries and studios to see works by Turkish artists. If you're lucky, you might catch an artist at work and learn about their techniques.

Afternoon

In the afternoon, participate in a traditional Turkish craft workshop. Learn the art of Ebru (paper marbling) or try your hand at making a Turkish carpet. These workshops provide a unique insight into Turkey's rich artistic traditions.

Evening

End your cultural immersion with a dinner at Alaturka Restaurant, where you can enjoy a mix of traditional and modern Turkish dishes while reflecting on your cultural experiences in Fethiye.

Adventure Seeker's Journey

Day 1: High Adrenaline Activities

Morning

Kickstart your adventure with a morning of paragliding over Ölüdeniz. The breathtaking views of the turquoise waters and rugged coastline from above are simply unforgettable.

Afternoon

After your exhilarating flight, head to Saklıkent Gorge for some canyoning. Navigate through narrow passages, jump into crystal-clear pools, and experience the thrill of this natural wonder.

Evening

For dinner, fuel up at Pasa Kebap, known for its hearty meals and energetic atmosphere. It's the perfect place to share stories of your day's adventures.

Day 2: Water Sports and Hiking

Morning

Spend your morning diving or snorkeling at Fethiye's top dive sites. Explore underwater caves, see vibrant marine life, and discover the beauty beneath the waves.

Afternoon

In the afternoon, tackle the Lycian Way, one of Turkey's most famous hiking trails. Choose a segment that fits your fitness level and enjoy the stunning views of the coast and mountains.

Evening

After a day of adventure, relax with a meal at Hilmi Restaurant. Located by the harbor, this restaurant offers fresh seafood and a relaxed atmosphere to wind down your day.

Day 3: Off-Road and On the Water

Morning

Start your final day with an off-road jeep safari. Explore the rugged terrain around Fethiye, visit hidden villages, and enjoy panoramic views of the countryside.

Afternoon

After your morning safari, spend the afternoon on a boat tour. Visit nearby islands, swim in secluded coves, and soak up the sun on the deck.

Evening

Wrap up your adventure trip with a dinner at Mancero Kitchen. This waterfront restaurant offers a great view of the sunset, the perfect backdrop for reminiscing about your adventurous journey in Fethiye.

Family-Friendly Adventures

Day 1: Fun and Relaxation
Morning

Start your family adventure with a visit to Sultans Aqua City. This water park is perfect for kids to splash around and enjoy various slides and pools, while parents can relax by the water.

Afternoon

After a fun-filled morning, head to Calis Beach for some relaxation. The shallow waters and gentle waves make it a safe place for kids to swim and play.

Evening

For dinner, visit Pizza Pepino. This family-friendly restaurant offers a variety of dishes, ensuring there's something for everyone, including delicious pizzas that kids love.

Day 2: Exploring Nature

Morning

Take your family to Butterfly Valley in the morning. Accessible by boat, this stunning location is home to a variety of butterfly species and offers a beautiful natural setting for a family hike and picnic.

Afternoon

In the afternoon, explore Saklıkent Gorge. The shallow waters and impressive scenery make it a fun and educational outing for children. There are also plenty of spots to sit and enjoy a packed lunch.

Evening

For dinner, head to Çarıklı Et Restaurant. Known for its grilled meats and friendly atmosphere, it's a great place for a hearty family meal after a day of exploration.

Day 3: Educational and Entertaining

Morning

Begin your day with a visit to the Fethiye Museum. The museum offers exhibits on local history and archaeology that can be fascinating for older kids and adults alike.

Afternoon

Spend your afternoon at the Fethiye Amusement Park. With a variety of rides and games, it's a perfect way to entertain the kids and let them have some fun.

Evening

End your family adventure with dinner at Yacht Classic Hotel Restaurant. This upscale restaurant offers a special kids' menu and a lovely view of the marina, making it a memorable dining experience for the whole family.

Budget Travel

Day 1: Affordable Exploration

Morning

Start your budget adventure with a visit to Fethiye Old Town (Paspatur). Walking through the historic streets and browsing the local shops costs nothing but offers a rich cultural experience.

Afternoon

Head to Calis Beach for a budget-friendly afternoon. The beach is free to access, and you can bring your own snacks and drinks to enjoy a relaxing day by the sea.

Evening

For an affordable dinner, try Megri Lokantası. This local eatery offers delicious Turkish dishes at reasonable prices, perfect for budget travelers.

Day 2: Nature and History

Morning

Spend your morning hiking a section of the Lycian Way. The trails are free to access and provide stunning views of the coastline and mountains.

Afternoon

Visit Kayaköy Ghost Town in the afternoon. The entrance fee is minimal, and exploring the ruins is a great way to learn about the local history without spending much.

Evening

For dinner, head to Pasa Kebap. Known for its affordable and hearty meals, it's a favorite among locals and budget travelers alike.

Day 3: Local Experiences

Morning

Begin your day at the Fethiye Market. Browsing the stalls and soaking up the lively atmosphere is free, and you can find inexpensive local snacks and souvenirs.

Afternoon

Spend your afternoon at Saklıkent Gorge. The entrance fee is low, and it's a wonderful place to explore the natural beauty of the region without breaking the bank.

Evening

End your budget travel experience with dinner at Mozaik Bahçe. This restaurant offers excellent value for money and a delightful garden setting to enjoy your meal.

This chapter offers tailored itineraries for different types of travelers, ensuring that everyone can enjoy the beauty and culture of Fethiye to the fullest. Whether you're here for a weekend getaway, seeking cultural immersion, adventure, family fun, budget travel, or a solo experience, Fethiye has something magical to offer.

Chapter 10

SHOPPING AND SOUVENIRS IN FETHIYE

Welcome to Fethiye's lively shopping scene, where every turn promises a unique find or a treasured memory. After spending several days exploring its lively markets, lovely boutiques, and secret artisan shops, I've accumulated a wealth of experiences and tips to share with other tourists. Whether you're looking for the perfect memento or simply want to immerse yourself in local culture, Fethiye's shopping scene is sure to captivate you. Let's explore the riches that lie in this enchanting Turkish town.

Local Handicrafts and Art

Unique Artisan Goods

One of the most enjoyable parts of Fethiye shopping is the availability of local handicrafts. There are numerous unique products that highlight the region's rich cultural past, ranging from finely woven carpets to wonderfully created ceramics. I've often found myself drawn to kiosks brimming with vivid textiles on my strolls through the markets. These aren't just any textiles; they're hand-loomed items that incorporate traditional Turkish patterns and techniques passed down through generations.

Ceramics and Pottery

Ceramics and pottery are another highlight. Turkish ceramics are visually stunning, with their vivid colors and detailed designs. I recall visiting a small workshop where the potter displayed the time-honored processes used to manufacture these stunning pieces. Seeing the process from start to finish gave me a new understanding for the craftsmanship involved. Whether you want a beautiful bowl, a conventional dish, or a magnificent vase, these ceramics make excellent mementos.

Jewelry and Accessories.

If you like jewelry, Fethiye will not disappoint. The local markets are packed with stalls selling everything from delicate silver pieces to bold, statement pieces embellished with semi-precious stones. One of my favorite finds was a handcrafted necklace made of turquoise, a stone that is both gorgeous and culturally significant in Turkey. Each piece of jewelry tells a story and serves as a lovely memento of your time in Fethiye.

Textile Treasures

Of course, no discussion of Turkish handicrafts is complete without discussing the breathtaking textiles. The selection is quite astounding, including hand-woven carpets, gorgeous kilims (flat-woven rugs), and luxurious silk scarves. Each piece showcases the weaver's talent and inventiveness. I remember buying a small kilim, and the intricate patterns and brilliant colors remind me of Fethiye's rich cultural tapestry.

Best Shopping Areas

Fethiye Market (Paspatur)

Fethiye Market, commonly known as Paspatur, is a great site to start your shopping trip. This old market area is a tangle of narrow alleyways dotted with stores and stalls that offer an incredible variety of things. From spices and sweets to clothing and accessories, you'll find almost anything here. The market has a vibrant atmosphere, with vendors shouting out to customers and the air scented with spices and fresh fruit.

Tuesday Market

If you're in Fethiye on Tuesday, don't miss the weekly market. This huge market encompasses a large portion of the town and is a sensory feast. It's a great place to buy fresh vegetables, local cheeses and olives, as well as textiles, clothing, and home items. I've spent several hours going through the stalls, conversing with vendors and trying delectable snacks. It's also an excellent place to hone your bargaining abilities!

Old town (Eski Kent)

The Old Town, often known as Eski Kent, is a superb shopping destination. You'll find a mix of classic and trendy boutiques, many set in attractive old houses. The narrow, cobbled alleyways are a delight to explore, and you never know what hidden gem you'll find. One of my favorite finds was a small shop that sold handcrafted soaps and natural beauty products, all prepared with care and attention to detail.

Local Bazaars

Don't pass up the smaller, local bazaars that may be found throughout Fethiye. These markets may not be as huge or well-known as the larger ones, but they offer a more intimate shopping experience and frequently have unique things that you won't find anywhere else. I've found some of my most prized keepsakes in these off-the-beaten-path markets, such as a gorgeously hand-painted ceramic bowl and a set of intricate brass candle holders.

Tips for Bargaining

- **Embrace Negotiation:** Approach negotiations in a nice and respectful manner. Begin by asking for the price, then make a lesser counteroffer and negotiate to find a mutually acceptable price.
- **Be Willing to Walk Away:** If the price isn't right and the vendor isn't willing to negotiate, say

thank you and walk away. This frequently causes the vendor to offer a lower price.
- **Build Rapport:** Engage with vendors by asking questions and showing genuine interest in their products. This generally results in better prices and a more satisfying experience.
- **Use Cash:** Vendors frequently prefer cash, especially in small markets. Carry small denominations to make transactions easier and sometimes more beneficial.
- **Practice Patience:** Take your time to explore and negotiate without rushing. Patience might lead to finding unique goods at lower pricing.
- **Learn basic phrases:** Using simple Turkish words like "Ne kadar?" (How much?), "Çok pahalı" (Too pricey), and "Teşekkür ederim" (Thank you) can improve your bargaining experience and demonstrate respect for the local culture.

Personal Experience and Recommendations

Memorable Finds

Over the years, I've discovered some genuinely noteworthy finds in Fethiye. One standout was a gorgeous, hand-painted porcelain platter that now proudly sits in my kitchen. The intricate design and brilliant colors never fail to attract the eye, and it serves as a lovely memento of my time in this great town. Another beloved item is a delicate silver bracelet set with turquoise stones, which I wear on special occasions.

Hidden Gems

Some of my finest shopping experiences have taken place in less well-known areas of Fethiye. Away from the bustle of the big markets, these hidden jewels can offer a more relaxing and private shopping experience. A small boutique nestled away in a quiet lane was one such discovery, where I found a selection of handmade leather journals. The quality and craftsmanship were amazing, and the shopkeeper was eager to share the story behind each piece.

Sharing Stories.

Shopping in Fethiye is more than just buying things; it's also about the stories and connections that come with each purchase. I've enjoyed numerous chats with vendors, learning about their crafts, lives, and passions. These conversations improved my travels and deepened my admiration for Fethiye's culture and traditions. Each object I've brought home contains a piece of these stories, making them even more special.

Practical Tips

Based on my experiences, here are a few practical tips for making the most of your shopping trip in Fethiye:

- **Start Early:** Especially during high tourist season, the markets can get crowded. Starting your shopping early in the day allows you to peruse at your pace while avoiding crowds.
- **Stay Hydrated:** Shopping in the hot Turkish weather can be exhausting. Make sure you bring a bottle of water and take breaks to stay hydrated.
- **Keep Your Belongings Safe:** Although Fethiye is typically safe, it is always a good idea to keep an eye on your goods, especially in crowded markets. A small crossbody bag or money belt can keep your things safe.
- **Ask for Recommendations:** Don't hesitate to ask locals or other travelers for their shopping recommendations. Personal tips and

suggestions are frequently the source of the best discovery and experiences.

Shopping in Fethiye is a journey unto itself, full of discovery, connection, and delight. Fethiye's markets and stores offer a wealth of treasures waiting to be discovered, whether you're looking for the perfect souvenir, a unique gift, or simply want to immerse yourself in the local culture. So take your time, taste the experience, and enjoy the quest of discovering that special treasure that will remind you of your time in this wonderful Turkish town.

Chapter 11

FESTIVALS AND EVENTS

Allow me to take you on a tour through the annual celebrations, cultural performances, and local festivities that bring life to this beautiful part of Turkey.

Annual Festivals

1. Fethiye Culture and Arts Festival

The Fethiye Culture and Arts Festival, held in late May or early June, is one of the year's highlights in Fethiye. This festival is a happy celebration of the local culture, art, and tradition. The streets are bustling with colorful parades, live music, dance performances, and art exhibitions. As someone who has firsthand experience with this festival, I can tell you that it is an excellent opportunity to immerse oneself in local culture and meet artists and performers who are enthusiastic about their craft.

2. Ölüdeniz Air Games Festival.

The Ölüdeniz Air Games Festival, held in October, is a must-see for adventure enthusiasts. Paragliders from around the world come in Ölüdeniz to show off their skills and execute stunning aerial acrobatics. The sight of colorful paragliders soaring above the beautiful Blue Lagoon is truly breathtaking. There are also courses and training sessions for people who want to experience paragliding for themselves. Believe me, watching these daredevils in action is an incredible experience.

3. International Ölüdeniz Dance Festival

The International Ölüdeniz Dance Festival, held annually in September, is another colorful event. This festival brings together dancers and troupes from several countries to perform both traditional and contemporary dances. The performances are held outdoors, frequently against the backdrop of the spectacular Ölüdeniz sunset. Whether you're a dance fanatic or simply a casual viewer, the intensity and grace of the dancers will captivate you.

Cultural Events and Performances

1. Traditional Turkish Night

Attending a Traditional Turkish Night is one of the greatest ways to experience Turkish culture. These events offer a great evening of Turkish music, traditional dance, and delicious cuisine and are held at various sites throughout Fethiye. The performers, clad in vivid costumes, perform traditional dances like as the whirling dervish and the belly dance. The rhythmic music and energetic ambiance provide an interesting and immersive cultural experience.

2. Classical Music Concerts at the Telmessos Theatre

The old Telmessos Theatre, with its breathtaking views of the sea, is both a historical site and a venue for classical music concerts. Consider listening to a wonderful symphony under the stars, surrounded by the historic remains of the theatre. These concerts are frequently held during the summer and feature talented musicians from Turkey and beyond. The combination of history, nature, and music results in a magnificent evening that you will not want to miss.

3. Local Folklore Performances

Fethiye has a significant folklore scene, and you may see local performances at numerous cultural centers and festivals. These performances feature traditional music, dances, and storytelling that reflect the region's heritage. One unforgettable experience I had was watching a folklore ensemble perform the Zeybek dance, a traditional Aegean dance known for its strong and heroic motions. The pride and passion of the dancers were extremely inspirational.

Public Holidays:

1. National Sovereignty and Children's Day (April 23)

Turkey celebrates National Sovereignty and Children's Day on April 23, a special holiday dedicated to children. In Fethiye, the day is marked by colorful parades, schoolchildren's performances, and a variety of kid-friendly events. The town is alive with excitement and laughter as families gather to celebrate. It's heartening to see the community's concern for the well-being and happiness of youngsters.

2. Republic Day (October 29).

Republic Day, October 29, marks the establishment of the Turkish Republic. Fethiye celebrates with a variety of events, including parades, concerts, and fireworks. The main square and streets are decorated with Turkish flags and decorations. The spirit of national pride is palpable, and this is an excellent opportunity to join the locals in commemorating their country's history and accomplishments.

3. Kurban Bayramı (Eid al-Adha)

Kurban Bayramı, also known as Eid al-Adha, is a major religious celebration in Turkey. It's a time for family get-togethers, feasts, and charitable activities. Traditional rituals such as animal sacrifice, which is subsequently shared with family, friends, and the less fortunate, may be seen in Fethiye. The event is marked by a sense of generosity and camaraderie, and visitors are frequently invited to join in the festivities.

Other noteworthy events:

1. Local Market Days

While not a traditional festival, Fethiye's weekly local markets are an event in their own right. Every Tuesday, the Fethiye Market transforms into a thriving center of activity, with sellers offering everything from fresh food to homemade crafts. The brilliant colors, alluring smells, and cheerful conversation make it a sensory feast. It's an excellent spot to experience local culture and get one-of-a-kind souvenirs.

2. Yacht Regattas.

Given its coastal location, Fethiye is a popular sailing destination, with various yacht regattas held throughout the year. These events draw sailors from all around the world and offer a spectacular spectacle of yachts racing across the turquoise waters. Whether you're an experienced sailor or simply like watching from the beach, the regattas lend a dash of excitement to Fethiye's marine charm.

3. Local Food Festivals.

Fethiye's culinary culture is honored through a variety of food festivals that emphasize local flavors and traditions. These festivals include food demos, tastings, and competitions. The Fethiye Mushroom Festival is one such event, where you can learn about the region's wild mushrooms while also sampling wonderful mushroom delicacies. Food festivals provide an excellent opportunity to sample local cuisine and discover new gastronomic delights.

Festivals and events in Fethiye offer a lively and dynamic look at the culture and traditions of the town. From colorful parades and dance performances to tranquil classical concerts and bustling markets, there is always something to pique your attention and imagination. Whether you're here for a specific festival or simply to experience local culture as it unfolds, Fethiye's festive energy will make your stay unforgettable. So, immerse yourself in the festivities, join the locals in their joyful rituals, and make unforgettable memories in this charming Turkish town.

Chapter 12

PRACTICAL INFORMATION

Traveling to a new location may be both thrilling and daunting, especially if it is your first time. Having spent a significant amount of time exploring Fethiye, I can provide a wealth of practical information to assist you navigate this lovely area of Turkey with ease and confidence. Let's get started with the fundamentals you need to know to make your vacation go smoothly and pleasurable.

Currency and Banking

Currency in Fethiye

Turkey's official currency is the Turkish lira. The majority of transactions, from buying souvenirs to dining out, will take place in lira. It's always a good idea to keep some local currency on hand for minor purchases, tips, and locations that don't accept credit cards.

Where to Exchange Money

Fethiye has numerous currency exchange offices (döviz) that offer competitive rates. These can be seen in tourist locations, in markets, and along the harbor. Most of them prominently display exchange rates, so it's worth looking around for the best offer. Banks also offer exchange services, but they may have slightly higher rates and lengthier wait times.

Using ATMs

ATMs are widely distributed in Fethiye and provide a handy option to withdraw cash. Look for machines from prominent Turkish banks, such as Garanti, İşbank, Akbank, and Ziraat Bank. Many ATMs have information in multiple languages, including English. Before using your card overseas, notify your bank to avoid problems with international transactions.

Credit and Debit Cards

Most hotels, restaurants, and larger shops take credit and debit cards. Visa and MasterCard are the most widely accepted, whereas American Express may be less so. It is usually a good idea to have some cash on hand for smaller places or in case of card machine malfunction.

Health and Safety Tips

Health precautions

Before you travel, you should check to see whether you need any vaccines or health precautions particular to Turkey. Generally, there are no mandatory vaccinations, but it's wise to be up-to-date with routine vaccines. A simple first aid bag with common drugs for headaches, gastrointestinal problems, and minor cuts is also recommended.

Tap Water

In Fethiye, it is preferable to drink bottled water over tap water. Bottled water is cheap and readily available in stores and supermarkets. To avoid stomach distress, use bottled water when brushing your teeth and making ice.

Sun Protection

Fethiye has a Mediterranean climate, with hot summers, thus sun protection is essential. Wear sunscreen with a high SPF, a hat, and sunglasses to protect yourself from the harsh sun. Staying hydrated is also important, so drink plenty of water, especially if you are out exploring.

Emergency Services

Turkey has an effective emergency response system. The main emergency number is 112, which will link you to ambulance, fire, and police services. It's helpful to know a few basic Turkish phrases, but most operators speak English. Fethiye State Hospital (Fethiye Devlet Hastanesi) is the major public hospital in case of an emergency, although there are also several private clinics and hospitals with English-speaking staff.

Travel Insurance

Why You Need It?

For any journey overseas, travel insurance is essential. It protects against unforeseen medical bills, trip cancellations, lost luggage, and other travel-related misfortunes. Given the variety of outdoor activities and adventure sports available in Fethiye, having comprehensive travel insurance ensures peace of mind.

Choosing A Plan

When choosing a travel insurance plan, search for one that covers medical emergencies, including evacuation, as well as adventurous sports like paragliding, scuba diving, and hiking. Check the policy provisions attentively to ensure that they cover all of the activities you plan to engage in.

Making a claim

Keep any pertinent receipts, medical reports, and police reports in case you need to make an insurance claim. Most insurance providers feature 24-hour helplines and online claim forms, making the procedure easier.

Communication and Internet

Mobile Phones

Using a mobile phone in Fethiye is simple. Ensure that your phone is unlocked, and consider purchasing a local SIM card for lower prices on calls, texts, and data. Turkcell, Vodafone, and Türk Telekom are the leading providers, with excellent coverage and a variety of prepaid plans.

Internet Access

Wi-Fi is widely available in Fethiye. Most hotels, restaurants, and cafes provide free Wi-Fi to its guests. If you need more devoted connection, internet cafes are an option. Buying a local SIM card with a data plan is a fantastic alternative for those who need continual access.

Power and Electricity

Voltage and Plugs

Turkey's supply voltage is 230V and the frequency is 50Hz. The plugs are types C and F, with two circular pins. If your equipment requires a different plug type, bring an adapter. Many hotels give adapters, but having your own is handy.

Device Charging

Most modern devices (laptops, phones, cameras) are compatible with 230V, but check your device specifications to be sure. Carrying a power bank can be beneficial, especially if you're out exploring all day.

Local Customs and Etiquette

Dress Code

While Fethiye is a popular tourist destination, it is nevertheless important to follow local customs. When visiting mosques or religious locations, dress modestly, including covering your shoulders and knees. Swimwear is permitted on the beach but not in town or public spaces.

Greetings

Turks are renowned for their hospitality. A popular greeting is a handshake, and it is courteous to use titles like "Mr." or "Mrs." with the person's first name. A small bow or nod is also an expression of respect.

Dining Etiquette

When dining, it is usual to start with a small appetizer (meze). When welcomed to someone's home, it is customary to bring a modest present, such as sweets or flowers. Wait for the host to start the meal at the table, and eat and pass food with your right hand.

Tipping Etiquette

Tipping is customary in Turkey, although not required. A tip of 5-10% is customary in restaurants where service is not included. Taxi drivers frequently round up their fares. Hotel employees, such as porters and housekeepers, typically earn a small tip for their services.

Service Charges

Some restaurants add a service charge (servis ücreti) to the bill. Check your bill to determine if this is the case; if not, giving a tip is a thoughtful gesture.

Respecting Traditions

Turkey has deep-rooted traditions. It's important to respect these practices. For example, when attending a mosque, take off your shoes and dress modestly. During Ramadan, avoid eating, drinking, or smoking in public areas during daylight hours to respect those who are fasting.

Photography Etiquette:

Always obtain permission before photographing people, especially in rural regions. Avoid photographing military installations or government structures. Check if photographing is permitted in mosques, and if so, practice discretion.

With this practical advice, you'll be ready to make the most of your time in Fethiye. These tips, whether it's about managing your money, staying well and safe, or honoring local customs, can help you navigate this lovely region with ease. In Fethiye, enjoy your trips, immerse yourself in the local culture, and make unforgettable experiences. Happy travels!

Chapter 13

WHAT TO DO AND NOT TO DO

Respecting Local Customs

Fethiye, like the rest of Turkey, has its own distinct customs and traditions. While the inhabitants are generally friendly and inviting, they appreciate tourists who respect their ways of life.

- **Greetings and Social Interactions:** When meeting someone, it is traditional to shake hands. If you're meeting someone you know well, a quick kiss on both cheeks is common. Always use your right hand for handshakes and when giving or receiving anything, as the left hand is considered less clean.
- **Dress Modestly:** It is especially necessary to dress modestly when attending religious institutions like mosques or cultural events. Women frequently cover their shoulders and knees. A lightweight scarf can be useful for

concealing your head when entering mosques. Men should avoid wearing shorts in these situations.
- **Respect Religious Practices:** If you hear the call to prayer, which occurs five times per day, be respectful. Avoid loud conversations or activities near mosques during prayer hours. If you visit a mosque, take off your shoes before entering, and if it's prayer time, stay silent.

Safety precautions

Safety is always a top issue when visiting, and Fethiye is a typically safe destination. However, like any major tourist destination, it is critical to remain careful.

- **Stay hydrated:** The Mediterranean temperature may be rather hot, especially during the summer. Bring a bottle of water with you and take rests in the shade to avoid heat exhaustion.
- **Watch Your Belongings:** Pickpocketing isn't a major issue in Fethiye, but it's always wise to keep an eye on your belongings. Use a money

belt or a lockable bag, and avoid carrying big sums of money.
- **Beach Safety:** Fethiye's beaches are gorgeous, although the currents can be powerful at times. Always follow local warnings and swim in permitted places. If you're not a strong swimmer, consider staying in shallower water.

Common Tourist Mistakes to Avoid

Every place has its eccentricities, and Fethiye is no exception. Here are some of the most common tourist blunders, along with tips for avoiding them.

- **Overpacking Itineraries:** Fethiye has so much to offer that it's natural to try to fit everything into your agenda. Take your time and enjoy every location and activity. It's preferable to completely experience a few things rather than rushing through many.
- **Ignoring Siesta Time:** Many stores and companies in Fethiye close in the afternoon for siestas. Plan your shopping trips and visits to local markets appropriately, and use this time to unwind and enjoy a leisurely lunch.

- **Tipping Incorrectly:** Tipping is appreciated in Fethiye but is not required. If service is not included in the bill, it is usual to tip 5-10%. Rounding up taxi fares is common practice.

CONCLUSION

Preparing for Departure

When the time comes to leave Fethiye, it can be bittersweet. I remember feeling a mix of satisfaction from all the adventures and a twinge of sadness that my journey was ending. Preparing for departure involves a few key steps to ensure everything goes smoothly. Let me guide you through it.

- Ensuring You've Packed Everything
- Settling Bills
- Returning Rental Items
- Saying Goodbye to New Friends

Nearby Destinations for Further Exploration

Leaving Fethiye does not have to be the end of your experience. The surrounding region is brimming with attractions that may simply be added to your agenda. Let's explore some excellent possibilities that I've personally visited and recommend at the end.

Dalyan

Dalyan, located just a short drive from Fethiye, is a tranquil town known for its natural beauty and historical significance. I spent a day cruising down the Dalyan River, seeing the ancient Lycian rock tombs cut into the rocks. The highlight for me was my visit to the Dalyan Mud Baths and Thermal Springs, where I had a great time covering myself in mud, which is reputed to have medicinal effects.

Patara

Patara is home to one of Turkey's longest beaches as well as numerous ancient ruin sites. I enjoyed touring the ancient city's ruins, which included the spectacular Roman amphitheater and the ancient parliament structure. The perfect way to unwind after taking up history was to lounge on the lovely sandy beach. Patara Beach is also a nesting area for loggerhead turtles, which will appeal to nature lovers.

Kas

Kas is a laid-back coastal town perfect for relaxing after a busy day in Fethiye. The town is famous for its clean waters and great diving spots. I spent a day diving in Kas and was captivated by the underwater landscape, which had shipwrecks and thriving marine life. The town itself boasts charming cobblestone lanes dotted with bougainvillea and tiny cafes where you can enjoy a leisurely supper.

Pamukkale

Pamukkale, widely known as the "Cotton Castle," is slightly further away but well worth the trip. The breathtaking white travertine terraces filled with warm, mineral-rich springs are a pleasure to see. Walking over these terraces was unreal, and the surrounding ancient city of Hierapolis added to the historical significance of the visit. Pamukkale's hot pools provide a one-of-a-kind experience that left me feeling revitalized.

Antalya

Antalya is a major city with a beautiful blend of historical sites and modern amenities. The old town of Kaleiçi, with its small lanes and historic residences, provides a delightful experience. I enjoyed visiting Hadrian's Gate and the Antalya Museum, which houses an excellent collection of artifacts. The city's beaches are also excellent, and if you have time, a boat trip down the Turquoise Coast is a must.

Planning Future Visits

Once you've fallen in love with Fethiye, you'll probably want to return. Start planning your future trip by making a list of places you missed or activities you'd like to explore. I have a trip journal in which I jot down thoughts and ideas for future visits. Returning to a favorite destination always results in a stronger relationship and fresh discoveries.

Sharing Your Experience

Share your trip experiences with friends and family. Your enthusiasm may encourage others to visit Fethiye and explore its delights. I've found that describing my exploits allows me to relive the delight and excitement of the trip. Furthermore, you may meet travel partners for your next adventure!

Supporting Local Businesses

You may support local companies in Fethiye even if you're not there. Purchase goods from local online merchants, such as handcrafted crafts or traditional Turkish items. This not only benefits the local economy, but it also allows you to enjoy a taste of Fethiye from home. I ordered tasty Turkish delights and lovely ceramics as gifts and for myself.

Learning the language

By learning some Turkish, you can strengthen your bond with Fethiye. Even simple sentences can go a long way toward making future journeys more enjoyable and engaging. There are numerous online resources, applications, and language classes available. During my visit, I found that speaking Turkish helped me interact with locals on a deeper level.

Volunteering and Giving Back

If you have a strong connection with Fethiye, try volunteering or participating in community projects. Many groups accept international volunteers for a variety of reasons, including environmental conservation, cultural preservation, and education. Giving back to a place that has given you so much is really satisfying.

Leaving Fethiye may mark the end of one adventure, but it paves the way for many more. Your journey does not have to come to an end, with neighboring destinations to explore and methods to stay connected. Enjoy the memories, share your experiences, and look forward to future travel. Fethiye has a way of catching your heart, and you'll find yourself wanting to return time and again. Until then, happy travels and may your adventures continue to be as fulfilling and joyous as those in Fethiye!

APPENDIX: USEFUL RESOURCES

Emergency Contacts

When traveling, it's crucial to have a list of emergency contacts readily available. In Fethiye, knowing who to call and where to go in case of an emergency can provide peace of mind and ensure a safe and enjoyable trip. Here are the essential contacts you should keep handy:

Police and General Emergencies

- Emergency Number (All Services): 112

This is the national emergency number for Turkey, connecting you to police, fire, and medical services.

Medical Assistance

Fethiye State Hospital (Fethiye Devlet Hastanesi)

- Address: Patlangıç, Ölüdeniz Cd., 48300 Fethiye/Muğla, Turkey

- Phone: +90 252 614 4017

Letoon Hospital

- Address: Foça Mah. Selahattin Sk. No: 10/1, 48300 Fethiye/Muğla, Turkey
- Phone: +90 252 612 6464

Police Stations

Fethiye Police Department

- Address: Patlangıç Mah. 107. Sk. No:1, 48300 Fethiye/Muğla, Turkey
- Phone: +90 252 614 4117

Coast Guard

- Coast Guard Command (Sahil Güvenlik Komutanlığı)
- Phone: 158 (direct line for maritime emergencies)

Embassy Contacts

It's wise to have the contact details of your country's embassy or consulate. Here are a few key contacts:

British Consulate in Fethiye

- Address: 508. Sk. No:6/1, 48300 Fethiye/Muğla, Turkey
- Phone: +90 252 614 6302

United States Embassy in Ankara (handles consular services for Fethiye)

- Address: Atatürk Bulvarı No: 110, Kavaklıdere, 06100 Ankara, Turkey
- Phone: +90 312 455 5555

Other Important Contacts

Tourist Information Center

- Address: Fethiye Marina, 48300 Fethiye/Muğla, Turkey
- Phone: +90 252 614 1516

Having these contacts saved in your phone or written down can save valuable time during an emergency.

Maps and Navigational Tools

Navigating Fethiye and its surrounding areas can be a breeze with the right maps and tools. Here are some resources that I found incredibly helpful during my travels:

Printed Maps

- **Fethiye Tourist Map:** Available at the Tourist Information Center, this map includes key attractions, hotels, restaurants, and transport hubs.
- **Lycian Way Hiking Map:** If you plan to hike the Lycian Way, a detailed trail map is essential. These maps can be purchased at local bookstores and outdoor gear shops.

Mobile Apps

- **Google Maps:** A reliable tool for navigating Fethiye, finding attractions, and getting directions. Offline maps can be downloaded for areas with limited internet access.

- **Maps.me:** Another great option for offline navigation. It offers detailed maps that include walking trails and lesser-known paths.

Online Resources

- **OpenStreetMap:** An open-source map that's detailed and regularly updated by contributors. Useful for exploring off-the-beaten-path areas.
- **Wikiloc:** An app and website where you can find user-uploaded hiking and biking routes around Fethiye and the Lycian Way.

Local Guides and Atlases

- **Fethiye City Guide:** Often available at hotels and the tourist center, this guide includes maps and useful information about the city.

Additional Reading and References

To deepen your understanding and enhance your experience in Fethiye, consider these additional resources:

History and Culture

- **The Lycian Way: Turkey's First Long-Distance Walking Route by Kate Clow:** A must-read if you're planning to hike the Lycian Way. It provides historical insights and practical hiking tips.
- **Turkey: A Short History by Norman Stone:** Offers a concise overview of Turkey's rich history, including the Lycian civilization that once thrived in the Fethiye region.

Online Articles and Blogs

- **The Culture Trip:** Features articles about Fethiye's attractions, local culture, and travel tips.
- **Nomadic Matt's Travel Site:** Provides budget travel advice and personal experiences about visiting Fethiye.

Academic and Historical Journals

- **Anatolian Studies:** A journal focusing on archaeological and historical studies in Turkey, including findings from the Fethiye region.

Reading up on these topics can provide a richer, more informed travel experience, allowing you to appreciate the history and culture of Fethiye more deeply.

Useful Local Phrases

While many people in Fethiye speak English, especially in tourist areas, learning a few basic Turkish phrases can enhance your experience and show respect for the local culture. Here are some useful phrases I found helpful:

Basic Greetings

- Hello: Merhaba
- Good morning: Günaydın
- Good evening: İyi akşamlar
- Goodbye: Hoşçakal (to the person staying), Güle güle (to the person leaving)

Common Courtesy

- Please: Lütfen
- Thank you: Teşekkür ederim
- Excuse me / Sorry: Affedersiniz

- Yes: Evet
- No: Hayır
- Essential Questions
- How much does this cost?: Bu ne kadar?
- Where is the bathroom?: Tuvalet nerede?
- Do you speak English?: İngilizce konuşuyor musunuz?
- Can you help me?: Bana yardım edebilir misiniz?

Directions

- Where is…?: …nerede?
- The beach: Plaj
- The hotel: Otel
- The restaurant: Restoran
- Left: Sol
- Right: Sağ
- Straight ahead: Düz
- At a Restaurant
- Menu: Menü
- Water: Su
- Tea: Çay
- Coffee: Kahve
- Bill: Hesap

Shopping

- Do you have…?: … var mı?

- I would like to buy....: ... satın almak istiyorum
- Can I get a discount?: İndirim yapabilir misiniz?

Emergencies

- Help!: Yardım!
- I need a doctor: Doktora ihtiyacım var
- Call the police: Polisi arayın

Learning these phrases can help you navigate interactions more smoothly and endear you to the locals. Even if your pronunciation isn't perfect, making the effort is always appreciated and can lead to more positive and enriching experiences.

This appendix should equip you with valuable resources, emergency contacts, navigational tools, further reading, and useful phrases to make your stay in Fethiye as seamless and enjoyable as possible. Happy travels, and may your journey be filled with wonderful adventures and lasting memories!

Printed in Great Britain
by Amazon